Business Etiquette

Business Etiquette

MARJORIE BRODY

BARBARA PACHTER

Business Skills Express Series

IRWIN
Professional Publishing

MIRROR PRESS

Burr Ridge, Illinois
New York, New York
Boston, Massachusetts

IRWIN
Concerned About Our Environment
In recognition of the fact that our company is a large end-user of fragile yet replenishable resources, we at IRWIN can assure you that every effort is made to meet or exceed Environmental Protection Agency (EPA) recommendations and requirements for a "greener" workplace.

To preserve these natural assets, a number of environmental policies, both companywide and department-specific, have been implemented. From the use of 50% recycled paper in our textbooks to the printing of promotional materials with recycled stock and soy inks to our office paper recycling program, we are committed to reducing waste and replacing environmentally unsafe products with safer alternatives.

Mirror Press:	David R. Helmstadter
	Carla F. Tishler
Editor-in-chief:	Jeffrey A. Krames
Project editor:	Jane Lightell
Production manager:	Ann Cassady
Interior designer:	Larry J. Cope
Cover designer:	Tim Kaage
Art manager:	Kim Meriwether
Compositor:	Alexander Graphics, Inc.
Typeface:	12/14 Criterion Book
Printer:	Malloy Lithographing, Inc.

Library of Congress Cataloging-in-Publication Data

Brody, Marjorie
    Business etiquette / Marjorie Brody, Barbara Pachter.
       p.   cm. — (Business skills express series)
    ISBN 0-7863-0323-9
    1. Business etiquette. I. Pachter, Barbara. II. Title.
  III. Series.
  HF5389.B76   1994
  395'.52—dc20

94–7620

Printed in the United States of America
1 2 3 4 5 6 7 8 9 0 ML 1 0 9 8 7 6 5 4

ABOUT THE AUTHORS

Marjorie Brody has been speaking, training, coaching, and writing professionally for more than 25 years. She is president of Brody Communications, Ltd., an international corporation which specializes in presentation
and business communication skills training and coaching. Ms. Brody has
worked nationally and internationally with executives from leading phar-
maceutical firms, the "big-six" accounting firms, and Fortune 100 and 500
companies. Among her clients are Merck and Company, Scott Paper Company, Towers Perrin, The University of Pennsylvania, SmithKline Bee-
cham, Colgate-Palmolive, The Vanguard Group, Johnson & Johnson, and
Price Waterhouse. Ms. Brody is a member of the American Society for
Training and Development, 3M Meeting Management Institute, the International Association for Continuing Education and Training, and the
National Speakers Association. Ms. Brody is coauthor of *Power Presenta-
tions: How to Connect with Your Audience and Sell Your Ideas* (John Wiley
& Sons, 1993).

Barbara Pachter is a speaker, trainer, and author known for her practical, results-oriented approach to building essential business communications and management skills. She is president of Pachter & Associates and
has designed and delivered hundreds of training programs for major cor-
porations and organizations around the world. These topics include business etiquette, business writing, presentation skills, communication skills,
women's seminars, and international awareness. Barbara Pachter has pre-
sented to a diverse range of companies, including 3M, AT&T, Abu Dhabi
Gas Company, Conrail, EPA, General Electric, Hewlett Packard, Johnson
& Johnson, Merck and Company, Merv Griffin Resorts Academy, Pruden-
tial, PSE&G, Recursos En Capacitacion LTDA., Rohm and Haas, Servistar
Corporation, and the US Department of Defense. A professional in the
field of business communications for more than 20 years, Ms. Pachter is

also coauthor of the *Complete Business Etiquette Handbook* (Prentice Hall). She is a member of the American Society for Training and Development and the National Speakers Association.

PREFACE

Have you ever wondered how to graciously handle a sticky situation at work? Did you ever feel uncomfortable because you weren't sure if you were behaving appropriately?

You're not alone. Many people feel unsure about appropriate business etiquette—social skills that are put to work in a business environment. *Business Etiquette* is a practical, easy-to-use book for everyone who wants to improve or polish his or her business manners.

As presenters of business etiquette seminars to employees throughout the United States, we understand your needs and concerns. This book teaches basic etiquette skills that enable you to feel confident and handle yourself appropriately, while treating others with respect and tact. Each chapter is devoted to a different aspect of business etiquette. Skills and techniques are clearly explained and valuable coaching tips appear throughout the book.

How can you get the most from this book? First, complete the Self-Assessment on page xv. Pay particular attention to your *almost never* responses and identify those areas where you need the most support.

Second, work through each chapter at your own pace. Try to complete one chapter at a sitting so that you can focus completely on a single topic.

Finally, take the Post-Test.

Once you complete this book, you can use it as a reference whenever you face an etiquette dilemma. Use the Skill Maintenance checklist on the inside back cover to ensure that you continue to practice all the techniques you have learned.

Good luck! You're on your way to improving your clout through courteous conduct.

Marjorie Brody
Barbara Pachter

About Irwin Professional Publishing

Irwin Professional Publishing is the nation's premier publisher of business books. As a Times Mirror company, we work closely with Times Mirror training organizations, including Zenger-Miller, Inc.; Learning International, Inc.; and Kaset International to serve the training needs of business and industry.

About the Business Skills Express Series

This expanding series of authoritative, concise, and fast-paced books delivers high-quality training on key business topics at a remarkably affordable cost. The series will help managers, supervisors, and frontline personnel in organizations of all sizes and types hone their business skills while enhancing job performance and career satisfaction.

Business Skills Express books are ideal for employee seminars, independent self-study, on-the-job training, and classroom-based instruction. Express books are also convenient-to-use references at work.

CONTENTS

Self-Assessment

Do you know how to behave? Specifically, do you know the proper protocol in a variety of business situations that require appropriate manners?

This self-assessment may confirm your confidence or suggest areas for improvement. In either case, it provides a starting point as you begin *Business Etiquette*.

	Almost Never	Sometimes	Usually	Almost Always
1. I feel confident giving and receiving compliments.	____	____	____	____
2. I know the proper way to introduce people.	____	____	____	____
3. I am considered a good listener.	____	____	____	____
4. I send thank-you notes within 24 hours.	____	____	____	____
5. I have no difficulty dressing appropriately for business situations.	____	____	____	____
6. I am not late for appointments.	____	____	____	____
7. I'm comfortable making small talk with new acquaintances.	____	____	____	____
8. I use the correct utensils at business lunches.	____	____	____	____
9. I know how to act at office parties.	____	____	____	____
10. I sound professional on the telephone.	____	____	____	____
11. If I'm bringing someone to my office, I know who opens the door and who enters the elevator first.	____	____	____	____
12. I act graciously when others demonstrate inappropriate manners.	____	____	____	____
13. My handshake sends a professional message.	____	____	____	____
14. When someone wants to speak with me, I make sure I don't stand too close or too far away.	____	____	____	____
15. I regularly evaluate my grooming routine to eliminate gaffes.	____	____	____	____

	Almost Never	Sometimes	Usually	Almost Always
16. I feel confident when presenting my business card.	_____	_____	_____	_____
17. I provide appropriate tips to waiters, waitresses, wine stewards, taxicab drivers, and hotel doormen.	_____	_____	_____	_____
18. I have a gracious manner when I transfer telephone calls or put people on hold.	_____	_____	_____	_____
19. I refill the paper and reset the copier after I use it.	_____	_____	_____	_____
20. I send faxes only with the recipient's advance approval.	_____	_____	_____	_____
21. When visiting another office, I wait for the host to indicate a chair before I sit down.	_____	_____	_____	_____
22. I give suitable gifts to co-workers on appropriate occasions throughout the year.	_____	_____	_____	_____
23. When entertaining clients, I dress and act appropriately.	_____	_____	_____	_____
24. I respect the privacy of other people's faxes and computer files.	_____	_____	_____	_____
25. I understand why manners matter.	_____	_____	_____	_____
Column totals:	_____	_____	_____	_____
Grand total: _____				

To score: Give yourself one point for each check under *almost never*, two points for *sometimes*, three points for *usually*, and four points for *almost always*. Total each column. Then add the totals of all four columns to get a grand total. How did you do?

100-90   Very good! You are a manners master.

89-75   Good. You are perceived as a polite person.

74-50   Average. You could improve your command of courteous behavior.

49-30   Poor. You need to learn and apply more etiquette skills.

29-0   Very poor. Your behavior will offend many people and needs improvement.

Business Etiquette

1 | Why Etiquette Excellence?

This chapter will help you to:

- Discover what business etiquette is, and what it isn't.
- Understand why business etiquette is important.
- Learn how business manners make a difference.

Four men and one woman are gathered for a board meeting when John K. Preston, the senior vice president, walks in. The four men stand up, approach Preston, say hello, and shake hands with him. The woman does not stand or approach Preston. He does not walk over to her. She nods and Preston nods back in acknowledgment. The meeting begins. ■

What message does this behavior send? Despite the reality of the situation, the woman does not seem to be on an equal footing with the men. An outside observer might conclude that she is neither as important as the men nor part of the team. And yet, both parties probably are doing what they were taught was correct behavior in social situations. The woman was probably taught that she doesn't need to stand when people enter a room nor does she need to shake hands. Preston may have been taught that men should wait for women to extend their hands in hand-shaking situations. In today's gender-equal workplace, however, their behavior may send an unintentional message.

When people talk about how they've been treated by a company or by an individual, often they're really talking about business manners. The

details—whether someone greets you in a courteous fashion, whether the person listens to what you have to say, whether that person deals with a complaint promptly—can determine whether a company gets repeat business.

Business etiquette puts social skills to work in business. Workplace manners give you confidence so that you can deal with people and situations in a polite, professional manner. You may be a whiz at your work, but if you insult people or dress inappropriately, your career suffers.

Describe a time when a co-worker was rude:

_____

_____

Describe a work situation in which you didn't know how to act appropriately:

_____

_____

Describe a difficult situation that someone handled well:

_____

_____

_____

MISSING MANNERS

Etiquette mistakes are all too common in today's business world.

Consider this list of common faux pas. Mark each one *(R)* for situations in which you were the *recipient* of impolite behavior, *(P)* for situations in which you *performed* the inappropriate action, or *(W)* for situations that you *witnessed*.

_____ 1. Answering a phone call during a meeting.

_____ 2. Wearing sloppy or inappropriate clothing.

_____ 3. Ignoring someone who just joined the group.

_____ 4. Borrowing a piece of equipment and not returning it promptly or in good condition.

_____ 5. Telling a dirty joke.

_____ 6. Barging into someone's office.

_____ 7. Chewing gum during a meeting.

_____ 8. Not looking at the person speaking.

_____ 9. Refusing to shake hands.

_____ 10. Using all the paper in the copier without refilling it.

_____ 11. Getting drunk at the company party.

_____ 12. Calling someone *babe* or *hon.*

_____ 13. Hanging up without apologizing when reaching the wrong number.

_____ 14. Standing too close to another person.

_____ 15. Interrupting someone's conversation.

In our fast-paced environment, we are not always aware that at some time we are all guilty of manners mishaps. Such mistakes may affect people's impressions of us and also may detract from the quality of life on the job.

Myths about Manners

Many people have misconceptions about the role of manners in the workplace. Complete this true-false test to assess your knowledge. Circle the correct response.

T   F   **1.** It takes more time to do things politely.

T   F   **2.** Guidelines for proper behavior just make things more complicated.

T   F   **3.** Etiquette is old-fashioned. Today, anything goes.

T   F   **4.** If an office has a laid-back environment, etiquette doesn't apply.

T   F   **5.** Manners are constant. Once you learn them, you don't have to update them.

T   F   **6.** If you get a reputation for being polite, people won't respect you.

T   F   **7.** Emphasizing what's proper just shows that you are a snob.

T   F   **8.** Manners stifle self-expression.

T   F   **9.** Manners won't help you improve the bottom line.

T   F   **10.** Business etiquette gives you firm rules, with the answer for every sticky situation.

Actually, all these statements are false. We'll explain why next.

1

THE EFFECTIVENESS OF ETIQUETTE

1. *It takes more time to do things politely.* False. While it may take time to learn to apply manners—just as it takes time to incorporate any new behavior into your routine—good manners save you time. You won't have to spend time soothing hurt feelings or making up for damaging mistakes.

2. *Guidelines for proper behavior just make things more complicated.* False. Etiquette isn't all that complicated. Most of the guidelines are based on kindness, efficiency, and logic. Once you become familiar with the guidelines, they're easy to apply. And, they free you from the discomfort of uncertainty and the fear of offending someone.

3. *Etiquette is old-fashioned.* False. While it's true that business today is not as universally formal as it once was, people still need to be courteous and act professionally. Not only does this reflect well on you and your company, but the work environment is also more enjoyable when people are kind and pleasant.

4. *If an office has a laid-back environment, etiquette doesn't apply.* False. Even if your office environment is quite casual and laid-back, etiquette is appropriate. Being friendly and polite is important in all environments.

5. *Manners are constant. Once you learn them, you don't have to update them.* False. While we often associate good manners with what our mothers told us about behaving in social situations, those rules don't always apply in modern business settings. For example, some women were taught to curtsy upon being introduced. And that is certainly not appropriate in today's work environment!

In addition, today's business environment is vastly different from the workplace of 20 or even 10 years ago, making it necessary to update the manners you learned earlier. Women, minorities, and people with disabilities have joined work environments that previously were the exclusive domain of white males. Today, it is a must to demonstrate sensitivity and eliminate behavior that might be considered sexist, racist, or discriminatory. A greater number of people with technical backgrounds are moving into positions in which they need strong interpersonal skills. In addition, more business is being conducted internationally, and what's proper in one culture may be offensive in another.

1

Manners also need updating to keep pace with technology, which has altered our methods of doing business. We frequently communicate by fax or voice mail; these useful but often impersonal tools actually increase the need for politeness.

6. *If you get a reputation for being polite, people won't respect you.* False. Being polite doesn't mean you'll lose clout—instead, you'll gain it. If you treat people with respect, they'll respect you. Aren't you more inclined to go the extra mile for someone who honors your dignity? Being strong doesn't have to imply being mean.

7. *Emphasizing what's proper just shows that you are a snob.* False. Sometimes, people do use their knowledge of protocol to intimidate others. However, being a snob actually demonstrates bad manners. The key to courtesy is making others feel comfortable.

8. *Manners stifle self-expression.* False. You can be yourself while being polite (unless, of course, you pride yourself on being rude). Good manners don't stifle self-expression—they just refine it. You can chitchat without engaging in malicious gossip. You can be honest without being crude. Etiquette allows for a wide range of behavior. You can be polite and still have plenty of personality.

9. *Manners won't help you improve the bottom line.* False. Applying appropriate business etiquette can both directly and indirectly enhance your company's bottom line. What's more, only a small investment is needed for a large return. Here's why: Customers and clients are more likely to do repeat business with a company that makes them feel comfortable and valued—two outcomes of appropriate business manners.

Within the organization, the application of etiquette skills improves morale and the quality of life while reducing turnover and improving efficiency. Employees who are treated politely feel valued and may be willing to contribute more.

A courteous demeanor can also advance your career and enhance your reputation as a professional. Poor manners place a ceiling on your advancement.

10. *Business etiquette gives you firm rules, with the answer for every sticky situation.* False. The guidelines that follow are neither rigid nor carved in stone. Appropriate behavior changes with the times and with the situation. While you should know and use good manners, you choose when to apply them. However, you certainly should not break etiquette guidelines out of ignorance. "A gentleman or a lady never does anything rude unintentionally," the old adage notes. The question to ask is, "If I'm not polite, what are the consequences to me?"

Business etiquette, of course, doesn't have an answer for every sticky situation. However, it can provide valuable guidelines that, combined with your knowledge of the circumstances and the personalities involved, will get you through most situations.

BENEFITS OF ETIQUETTE

Being aware of appropriate business etiquette can benefit you in many ways:

1. Good manners help you make a positive impression.
2. Being perceived as a professional enhances your credibility.
3. Knowing that you are behaving appropriately helps you feel relaxed and confident so you can focus on business.
4. Following the protocol of being polite shows that you are a team player.
5. People like to do business with you when you make them feel comfortable.

These benefits apply in a variety of situations. They're equally useful when . . .

- You're going to present a report to the head of your division.
- You've been invited to dinner at your supervisor's home.
- Because of restructuring, everyone's workload has increased.
- A prospective client is coming to your office for a meeting.

List any other situations in which etiquette awareness assists you:

_____

_____

_____

In today's business environment, our products and services are not all that different from those of others. What distinguishes us is what we bring to our business relationships. When you treat others with respect and kindness, you demonstrate the kind of etiquette that benefits your business.

Chapter Checkpoints

✓ The rules of appropriate business etiquette have changed as the workforce has expanded and as technology has become more sophisticated.

✓ Business etiquette skills increase your confidence and clout.

✓ Appropriate business manners benefit you individually as well as your company collectively.

2 | Manners for Meeting and Greeting

This chapter will help you to:

- Make appropriate introductions.
- Know when, and how, to shake hands.
- Present your business card in an effective fashion.

Robin Thompson, a partner in an accounting firm, went to meet with her client, Gregory Tavistock, in his office. After shaking hands, Greg asked Robin to sit down. In that split second, however, Greg also realized that following his morning swim, he had left his wet swimming trunks on the back of his chair.

Embarrassed, Greg quickly shouted, "Wait!" and snatched his trunks from the chair. Unfortunately, there was no other available chair, so Robin, thanks to the dripping trunks, still had a wet seat. ■

How we greet people has a strong influence on how they perceive us. First impressions can be lasting ones. These short yet highly significant encounters can set the tone for the entire interaction that follows. If you make a poor initial impression, you may spend the rest of your meeting trying to overcome it.

Describe how you'd feel if someone greeted you in the manner indicated:

2

Client stands to greet you, shakes hands, offers a chair, and addresses you by name. _____

_____

Colleague continues to talk on the phone as you enter his office and doesn't motion for you to sit down. _____

_____

Supervisor fails to introduce you to a person you don't know as you join the group. _____

_____

Supervisor introduces you to a new client while adding some flattering descriptions of your professional expertise. _____

_____

Colleague fails to shake hands with you as you extend yours.

_____

_____

IMPRESSIVE INTRODUCTIONS

Making introductions can feel awkward, but that's no reason to avoid them. When someone is not introduced, people feel uncomfortable or distracted; they may not fully concentrate on the conversation as they try to figure out who the stranger is. Guessing who the other person is can be downright dangerous. She could be the reclusive vice president, a vendor, or a cousin stopping by to visit a co-worker.

So the most important thing you can do about introductions is to remember to make them! When people know who the players are, they can focus on their roles in the game.

Here is an ABC of introductions, which should get you through most situations:

A = Authority. Say the name of the person who holds the position of most authority or importance first. This applies regardless of gender and age. For example, "Ms. Manager, I'd like you to meet Mr. New Employee."

B = Basic. Keep it basic. You have to say each person's name only once. Avoid the back-and-forth ping-pong of introducing everyone to each other. (You don't need to say, "Ms. Manager, meet Mr. New Employee. Mr. New Employee, meet Ms. Manager.")

C = Clarify. If you can, provide some information about the people you are introducing. For example, "Ms. Manager, I'd like you to meet Mr. New Employee. He comes to us from Amalgamated Consolidated, where he worked for five years. Ms. Manager has been our head of marketing since last January."

Smoothing over Sticky Situations

Of course, not all introductions go smoothly. Here are some problems that come up occasionally during introductions. Check off those situations that you have experienced:

_____ Didn't know whether to use person's first name or title (Dr., Mrs., Ms., Miss, Mr.).

_____ Forgot the name of the person you were introducing.

_____ Guessed at a name and used the wrong one.

_____ Didn't know which person to introduce first.

_____ Wondered what to do when someone didn't introduce you.

_____ Didn't know whether to stand up or shake hands when introduced.

_____ Wasn't sure how to respond to an introduction.

Common sense, combined with courtesy, can help you through most of these situations. Here are some general guidelines for handling sticky situations:

2

When in doubt, don't use first names. It's always better to use Mr., Ms., or Dr. until you're asked to use first names or are sure that it's appropriate to do so. Ms. is often the preferred title for women.

If you don't know or if you forget the name of the person you are introducing, admit it! While it's possible to guess, you'll feel embarrassed if you use the wrong name. Just admit that you forgot. This happens to everyone sooner or later. You can say something like, "I'm terribly sorry, but my mind's gone blank and I've forgotten your name."

If someone neglects to introduce you, possibly because of a memory lapse, go ahead and introduce yourself. Say, "Hello, I'm Julie Gordon. I don't believe we've met."

When you are unsure which person has the position of most authority or importance, or if everyone's position is equal, choose the person you wish to compliment and mention that person first. When in doubt, you can fall back on traditional rules, which would compliment the elder person or the female.

When you are introduced, stand up and shake hands. Women should do this too, despite what they may have been taught by their mothers or grandmothers. If you are trapped in a chair or otherwise unable to stand, indicate that you would if you could. Move toward the person you're meeting, establish eye contact, look pleasant, and smile. Repeat the name of the person you've just met. Say something like, "Pleased to meet you, Kira," or "Hello, Ms. Ford."

Introducing Yourself

In case you are not introduced or no one is available to introduce you, have a self-introduction—a planned and practiced way of describing who you are or what you do—that is clear, interesting, positive, and well delivered. This introduction is your own 10-second commercial, a way to provide essential information and help start a conversation. You can tailor your introduction to the event.

Some examples: "Hi. I'm Ross Herman. I'm a management consultant for the ABC Company, specializing in strategic planning."

"Hello. I'm Nathan Westminister. I'm an administrative assistant for the senior vice president at XYZ Company."

"Hello. I'm Sue Haddon, the office manager for the Philadelphia office."

Write your own self-introduction:

_____

_____

_____

Now, try saying your self-introduction out loud. Practice in front of a mirror until you are comfortable.

HANDLING THE HANDSHAKE

In the currency of business encounters, the handshake is the dollar—the most frequently exchanged legal tender of American business transactions. As the most common of all forms of greetings, the handshake is a traditional sign of trust. In the past, extending your hand in friendship demonstrated that you were unarmed.

Today, the handshake is an important symbol of respect, the most important aspect of the proper protocol for business greetings. Whether you are male or female, to be taken seriously, you must shake hands appropriately. You want your handshake to give you the respect you deserve.

Some handshakes send the wrong signals. Match the type of handshake with the meaning often attached to it.

_____ 1. Limp handshake.

_____ 2. Bone-crushing handshake.

_____ 3. Two-handed handshake, in which a hand is placed on top of the one being shaken.

_____ 4. No response to extended hand.

_____ 5. Sweaty palms.

A. The person is aloof.

B. The person is nervous.

C. The person is a wimp.

D. The person is trying to dominate you.

E. The person is acting too familiar or trying to establish power.

Practical Practice

Getting a Grip on Reality

Pay attention to the handshakes of people you regularly encounter. Do the handshakes confirm what you know about these people professionally, or do the handshakes conflict with your image? Seek feedback on your own handshake from a trusted acquaintance. What message does it send?

How to Shake Hands

The following three steps can help you improve your handshake:

1. *Say your name and extend your hand.* Usually the higher-ranking person should extend a hand first, but if he or she doesn't, you should. Because it used to be considered polite for a man to wait for a woman to extend her hand, many people are confused on this point. For this reason, a woman may want to extend her hand first—just in case the man is waiting for it.

2. *Extend your hand at a slight angle, with your thumb up. Touch thumb joint to thumb joint.* Put your thumb down gently once contact has been made, and wrap your fingers around the palm of the other person's

Answers: 1-C, 2-D, 3-E, 4-A, 5-B

hand. (Many people think they already use this technique but are surprised to find that it feels different from their usual handshake.)

3. *Provide a firm handshake but not a bone-breaking one.* About two or three pumps are enough.

You should greet disabled people in the same polite fashion that you would anyone else. You might ask a blind person, "Shall we shake hands?" You might extend your left hand if the person has an artificial right hand.

2

■ **T i p s** ───────────────────

Handling Handshake Problems

When you are the recipient of a poorly executed handshake, remain courteous and don't draw attention to the other person's behavior. Here's how to deal with some specific handshake faux pas and problem situations:

Failure to offer a hand in response to yours: Just put your hand down and carry on.

A limp handshake: Aim for the thumb joint. This position will eliminate some of the limpness.

A bone-crushing handshake: Go limp. Holding your hand at a slight angle should reduce the pressure.

A drink or briefcase is in your handshaking hand: When you're in a situation in which you can reasonably expect to shake many hands, hold your drink or other items in your left hand. If you get caught holding something, transfer the item and then shake hands.

Sweaty palms: Use a cotton handkerchief or talcum powder.

When to Shake Hands

Knowing *when* to shake hands is just as important as knowing *how* to shake hands.

Check off those situations in which you think you should regularly shake hands.

_____   When you are introduced to someone.
_____   When you say goodbye to someone.

_____   When someone from the outside (a client, customer, vendor, or visitor) enters your office.

_____   When you see someone you haven't seen in a long time, such as a co-worker from another division.

_____   When you enter a meeting and are introduced to the participants.

_____   When a meeting ends.

_____   When you encounter a business colleague outside the office.

_____   When you feel it is appropriate.

Actually, all of these situations are suitable handshake moments—times at which it's customary and courteous to shake hands.

BUSINESS CARD BASICS

Business cards do not belong in a box in your desk drawer. They don't do you any good there. Business cards were made to be exchanged.

Describe the last three times you gave someone your business card or someone gave a business card to you:

1. _____
   _____

2. _____
   _____

3. _____
   _____

Your card represents you and should provide a professional image. It should be well designed and printed on quality paper. Make sure it's not too busy with extra information and graphics. The most important

2

information it should include is your name, your title, your address, and your phone number. Even if your company provides you with a card, you might want to invest in a specialized card that emphasizes your professional, rather than your corporate, affiliations.

In the United States, the proper way to exchange business cards is relatively simple. Here's a checklist you can use to determine if your technique is appropriate. You should be able to answer yes to all the questions.

☐ *Is your card in good shape—not tattered, folded, or flimsy?*

☐ *Is your card readily available?* You shouldn't have to fumble around in your purse or briefcase. Always keep the cards in the same place to make them easier to find. The inside pocket of your suit or a jacket pocket is a good location.

☐ *Are you selective about distributing your cards?* You don't want to hoard your cards, but neither do you want to hand them out indiscriminately. You devalue them by doing so. Ask yourself whether someone might actually want the card to contact you in the future. It's better to err *slightly* on the side of excess distribution.

☐ *Are you presenting your card at an appropriate time?* Just before you part company with someone you have just met for the first time may be a good time to exchange cards. In a group situation, you may distribute your card at the beginning of the meeting. Don't hand out your card during a meal. Wait until afterwards.

☐ *When appropriate, do you personalize the card by adding your home phone number in pen?* It's more effective to write your phone number down in front of a recipient than to have it printed on the card.

> ■ **Tip** ─────────────────────────────
>
> ## Name Tag Tip
>
> Frequently at conventions or conferences, you receive a name tag as a means of identification. The proper placement is high on your right shoulder. This position makes your name tag more visible to someone shaking your right hand.

Gracious Greetings

Meeting someone is like the opening of a play—the rest of your performance and perhaps even the length of your run are measured against the impression you make in those first few seconds. You can get off to a good start by shaking hands appropriately, making polite introductions, and presenting your business card in a professional manner and at the appropriate time.

Chapter Checkpoints

✓ The most important point about introductions is to remember to make them!

✓ Mention the name of the person holding the position of most authority or importance first during introductions. Keep introductions basic. Clarify with additional information when possible.

✓ When meeting someone for the first time, stand, say your name, and shake hands.

✓ Provide business cards that are well designed and in good shape, personalizing them with your home phone number if the situation calls for it.

3 | Successful Encounters

This chapter will help you to:

- Become more comfortable when you make small talk.
- Learn how to listen so that other people feel that they are heard.
- Implement techniques to stay on schedule.

Michelle Sisko loved her job, but she hated Monday mornings because each followed a predictable pattern. No sooner would she step off the elevator than she would be approached by Kyle Maxwell, an ambitious junior executive who was eager, even desperate, to engage her in conversation. Michelle wouldn't even have her coat off before Kyle would greet her with a rhetorical "Hi. How 'ya doing?" and then launch into a soliloquy: "You know, I've been thinking about those marketing plans, and I've come up with the answer."

Kyle never wasted time engaging in the pleasantries of small talk. He also never came up for air or allowed Michelle to interject a word. He followed Michelle as she hung up her coat, opened her briefcase, and tried—all too often in vain—to get organized for the Monday morning staff meeting. Kyle never understood why he was repeatedly passed over for promotion. ■

Every encounter offers an etiquette opportunity—a chance to impress the other person with your gracious demeanor. Whether a new acquaintance or someone you deal with every day, that person's perception of you is influenced by your conversational and listening skills as well as by your demonstration of respect for that person's time.

Match the following behaviors with the impressions they create:

Behavior	Impression Created
_____ 1. Talks too much	A. Efficient
_____ 2. Ignores others	B. Too serious
_____ 3. Interrupts	C. Snobbish
_____ 4. Only discusses work	D. Nervous or insensitive
_____ 5. Meets deadlines	E. Rude

SMALL TALK SKILLS

Small talk may seem unimportant, but it has a potentially huge impact on how others respond to you. It contributes to your credibility and your ability to establish rapport; it also helps set clients at ease. If you work for a large company, small talk may offer the only way to connect with people in other departments. In addition, it may be a way to build a bridge of communication with your superior.

List three work situations in which you are expected to engage in small talk:

1. _____

_____

2. _____

_____

Answers: 1–D, 2–C, 3–E, 4–B, 5–A

3. _____

_____

   The ability to effectively engage in small talk includes three key components: tuning-in techniques, listening manners, and acting appropriately when it's your turn to talk.

Tuning-In Techniques

The first step for success in small talk is readying yourself to listen. The second step is letting others know that you are paying attention to them. The acronymn SOFTEN explains how to show someone you are paying attention.

   S = _Smile._ A smile is a sign of friendliness and receptivity.

   O = _Open posture._ Appear attentive and face the speaker. Don't cross your arms or legs.

   F = _Forward lean._ Leaning forward shows that you're alert. However, don't invade the other person's space. Stay about an arm's distance away.

   T = _Tone._ Make your tone of voice show interest. In addition, don't mumble, shout, or whisper.

   E = _Eye contact._ Look directly at the speaker without staring.

   N = _Nod._ Nodding indicates agreement or just understanding of what is said. Be careful not to nod too much.

   These body-language basics let you communicate without saying a word. Through posture, eye contact, and gestures, you are telling people that you are receptive to what they have to say. You can use these cues to signal that you are ready for conversation. Or, by omitting them, you show that you are temporarily too rushed, overloaded, or otherwise unable to talk at the moment. You should also pay attention to these cues in the body language of others, just as Kyle should have learned how to better read Michelle.

Label the following body-language signals. Use *(P)* for those that create a *positive*, polite impression and *(N)* for those that give a *negative*, impolite impression—mannerisms that can signal someone isn't giving the speaker full attention. Ask yourself whether you regularly exhibit any of the behaviors labeled *N*.

_____ **1.** Tapping feet   _____ **8.** Head and chin up

_____ **2.** Arms at side   _____ **9.** Shifting feet

_____ **3.** Hanging head   _____ **10.** Looking away

_____ **4.** Swaying   _____ **11.** Feet still

_____ **5.** Shoulders relaxed   _____ **12.** Crossed arms

_____ **6.** Hands in pockets   _____ **13.** Hands on hips

_____ **7.** Direct eye contact   _____ **14.** Slouching

Practical Practice

I See What You Mean

Ask someone to videotape you during a routine conversation after getting permission from the other person or persons involved. Turn off the sound and play back the tape. Rate yourself on your body language. What can you improve?

Listening Manners

We have two ears and one mouth for a good reason: We should listen twice as much as we speak! Listening involves actively tuning in to what the other person has to say. You can get ready to listen in these ways:

- *Create a setting in which you can listen.* You may need to close the door, hold telephone calls, or sit next to the person who is speaking.

Answers: 1–N, 2–P, 3–N, 4–N, 5–P, 6–N, 7–P, 8–P, 9–N, 10–N, 11–P, 12–N, 13–N, 14–N

- *Tune out internal distractions.* You might be feeling hungry, have a headache, or even be wondering how to deal with your difficult co-worker. However, you won't really hear what the other person is saying if you think about those things instead of what she's telling you.
- *Monitor your body language.* If you're frowning, fidgeting, or staring into space, you're sending signals that tell the speaker you're not receptive.

3

At times, we all fall into poor listening habits. Check off any of the following scenarios that describe how you sometimes half-listen to people:

————— I tune out information that is too difficult or technical to understand.

————— I get distracted by visual images—a person's facial expressions, gestures, dress, or posture—and miss the message.

————— I let my mind wander, especially when the other person speaks slowly.

————— I can't wait to share my thoughts, so instead of listening, I think about what I want to say.

————— I take what is said literally, without paying attention to the tone of voice, facial expression, or situation in which the statement is being made.

————— I listen only for information that I can challenge, like a cross-examining attorney.

Active listening involves not only tuning into what someone is saying but also letting the speaker speak and then reflecting back the person's words. If you interrupt, finish someone's sentences, or think about what he or you might say next, you won't fully communicate. You need to repeat or paraphrase what was stated, ask questions that clarify the comments, and offer words of encouragement or acknowledgment. Only after you've completed these steps is it your turn to talk.

3

Practical Practice ———————————

I Hear You

Place a tape recorder on the table during a family dinner or tape-record part of a lunch discussion with a friend who grants permission. Let the machine run long enough for you to forget it is there.

Play back the tape. Give yourself one point for each time you do any of the following:

- Offer words of encouragement: "I see."
- Repeat or paraphrase what the person said: "So what you're saying is . . ."
- Ask a clarifying question: "Could you elaborate on that?"
- Prompt the person to continue: "That's interesting. Tell me more!"

Subtract one point for each time you interrupt, finish a sentence, change the subject, offer an unsolicited opinion, or disagree before letting the person know you've heard what's been said.

Make sure the conversation is long enough for you to realistically practice the skills. A low or negative score means you need more practice to perfect your listening skills.

Your Turn to Talk

While it's usually appropriate to respond to what someone else has said, it's also a good idea to have a repertoire of topics that you feel comfortable bringing up. You can find things to talk about by paying attention to current events, the weather, the world around you, and developments within your industry.

On the following lines, write something pleasant you could say in one sentence about each of the following safe, small-talk topics:

The weather: _____

_____

Sports: _____

_____

Traffic: _____

_____

Business events: _____

_____

Books, movies, TV shows: _____

_____

Meeting place or city: _____

_____

Some topics, of course, should be avoided during casual conversations. It's best not to discuss topics like the following:

- Your health or someone else's health.
- Personal misfortunes.
- Income.
- Stories of questionable taste, dirty jokes, or gossip.
- Religion and highly controversial issues such as abortion.
- Intimate details about your personal life.

Describe a time when someone discussed something that made you feel uncomfortable: _____

_____

_____

3

■ Today's Topic Is...

Each day for a week, come up with a small-talk topic of the day. Try each topic out on a friend or acquaintance (waiter or waitress, store clerk, garage attendant).

At the end of each day, grade yourself from A to D on the success of each topic. Base the grade on your knowledge of the topic, your comfort in discussing it, the kind of response it received, and whether you would use a similar topic again. Fill out this report card:

	Topic	Grade
Monday	_____	_____
Tuesday	_____	_____
Wednesday	_____	_____
Thursday	_____	_____
Friday	_____	_____

Now, put the topic in a category: sports, business events, weather, and so on. List the category that received the best grade during the week, followed by the next successful category, and so on.

	Category
1. *Most successful:*	_____
2. *Next successful:*	_____
3. *Next successful:*	_____
4. *Next successful:*	_____
5. *Least successful:*	_____

> **Hint**
>
> How many times do you speak to someone without addressing that person by name? Although it's easy to fall into the habit of just using *you* or skipping names altogether, it is much more effective and gracious to call someone by name.
>
> Next time you make small talk with someone, interject that person's name into the conversation at least once.

Opening Lines

For many people, the most difficult part of any conversation is the beginning. We've found that four categories of opening lines work well. Each of the following four categories contains an example. On the lines below each category, write an example of your own.

1. *Upbeat observation:* "This is an impressive facility. It looks as if a lot of thought went into its design."

_____

_____

2. *Open-ended question:* "What's your impression of this conference so far?"

_____

_____

3. *Pleasant self-revelation:* "I just started going to graduate school."

_____

_____

4. *General question:* "Where are you from?" or "How long have you worked for MBP Group?"

_____

_____

3

TIPS ON TIMING

Part of making the most of every encounter is showing respect for the other person by honoring the schedule. This means being on time and limiting meetings to their stipulated length.

Appointments are not approximations. It's rude to be late. Being late implies that you think your time is more valuable than the other person's. That person may become insulted and decide to take his or her business elsewhere. What's more, when you arrive at a location rushed and anxious, you need even more time to settle down and focus on business.

Describe a time when being late had a negative impact on you or on a co-worker: _____

_____

_____

_____

Sometimes, of course, events beyond our control make us late. In that case, it's best to tell people about the problem and adjust the schedule.

If you are the host, let a visitor know that you are running behind schedule. Depending on the length of the delay, the visitor may want to wait, come back, or reschedule. If the wait will be short, offer a beverage to help the person pass the time. Show the visitor to a reception area that has comfortable chairs and a few magazines to read.

If you are the visitor and will be delayed by more than 10 minutes, call to let your host know. Give that person the option of canceling or rescheduling the meeting. Apologize for your delay when you arrive.

Of course, there are many things you can do to avoid being late. Check any of the following items that you need to do more frequently:

_____   Schedule meetings farther apart so that if one runs over, the next meeting won't be delayed.

     _____   Better estimate how long something really takes.

     _____   Be more organized: Leave earlier, assemble materials in advance, plan the route.

     _____   Schedule fewer tasks into each day rather than planning more than you can reasonably accomplish.

     _____   Set your watch, office clock, and car clock five minutes ahead so that you can be "late" and also be on time.

3

List any other strategies you can think of:

_____

_____

_____

It's also important that you don't overstay your welcome. Whether you are visiting a co-worker's office to discuss a problem or making a sales presentation to a prospective client, don't stay longer than the business requires. Leaving on time is just as important as arriving on time.

Meeting the Schedule for Meetings

"At meetings," someone once said, "you take minutes and waste hours." The fact is, meetings do take up a lot of time; however, you can use techniques to make them more efficient and productive.

The basic question a meeting planner should ask is, "Is this meeting really necessary?" Perhaps the business of the meeting could be accomplished by another means: a phone call, a memo, a notice on the bulletin board, or just a decision made on your own!

The first two questions any meeting participant should ask are, "Do I really need to go?" and "Do I need to be there for the entire meeting?" Perhaps you could attend only the portion of the meeting that relates to your work. (If you are planning a meeting, it is gracious, where feasible, to give participants the option of attending for only a portion of the meeting and to plan the agenda around their schedules.)

3

A GREAT IMPRESSION

In the work world, often we don't get a chance to know people well. Our encounters are, in most instances, focused on the business at hand. We want to make what little time we do have count for us by establishing our images as courteous professionals. By engaging in appropriate small talk, listening attentively to what people have to say, and demonstrating respect for people's time, we'll have communicated effectively through the subtle shorthand of good business etiquette.

Chapter Checkpoints

✓ Listening attentively to someone is a way to make that person feel valued and respected.

✓ The ability to make small talk contributes to your reputation as a courteous professional.

✓ You can prepare for spontaneous conversations by having a repertoire of topics to discuss.

✓ Arriving on time and staying on schedule are signs of respect. It's important to show that you value another person's time.

4 | Spatial Arrangements
Three-Dimensional Diplomacy

This chapter will help you to:

- Graciously manage doors and elevators.
- Understand taxicab courtesy.
- Handle office seating cordially.
- Maintain appropriate space between people.

Brittany Melrose, a human resources manager, asked Jasmine Downs, the benefits supervisor, to explain what took place during a meeting that she couldn't attend. Jasmine stopped by her office to do so, and Brittany rose to greet her.

Before Brittany could invite Jasmine to sit down, Jasmine launched into a lengthy description of a controversy during the meeting. In agitation, she paced and gestured while rehashing the argument, stepping closer to Brittany every time she shared a confidential opinion about the matter. Each time she approached, Brittany took a step back, but Jasmine, by now caught up in the story, didn't pay attention to her own body language, or to Brittany's. By the time Jasmine stopped talking, Brittany literally had been backed up against the wall. ■

Space may be the final frontier for courtesy—that arena where etiquette must be appropriate in three dimensions and even while someone is in motion. Yet many people spin out of orbit when it comes to graciously handling exits and entrances, traveling by taxicab, setting up office seating, and determining how close is too close when talking with someone.

■ Manners in Motion

Examine the following list. Mark a check beside any situations in which you don't know the proper protocol:

_____ Who exits an elevator first.	_____ Whether to walk a visitor to the elevator.
_____ How to hail a cab.	_____ Who enters an elevator first.
_____ How to enter a revolving door.	
_____ Whether to greet someone in a crowded elevator.	_____ Whether to hold the door.
	_____ Whether to sit down when visiting someone's office.
_____ Where to stand in relation to someone else.	_____ Who goes through a doorway first.

INS AND OUTS: DEALING WITH DOORS

Behaving appropriately around doors isn't always an open-and-shut case, but that's no reason to become unhinged. In the past, many rules about who opened the door, who held it, and who went through first were based on gender or on the relative status of the two individuals (such as supervisor or employee). Today, door decisions swing more toward practicality.

The basic guideline is whoever gets to the door first opens it. This guideline applies regardless of gender, corporate position, or age. In some situations, such as escorting a visitor, the host should try to get to the door first and hold it for the guest.

It's polite to help anyone who needs help, regardless of gender or age. For instance, if someone is carrying something and you can assist by opening the door, do so.

Whether a woman should hang back so a man can open the door or whether a junior member of the team should hustle to open the door for an executive depends both on your personality and on your corporate climate. If you or your business environment are traditional, it may work best to follow the more traditional rules—having the man hold the door for the woman or the younger person open the door for the senior one.

It's also gracious to allow people to save face—to avoid putting them in positions that make them uncomfortable. If an older man would become upset when a woman doesn't allow him to hold a door, the woman should permit him to do so. The reverse is equally true: If a woman would become self-conscious while a group of men waited for her to go through a door first, the men should just walk through in order of arrival.

Naturally, it's always polite to hold the door for someone, especially if his hands are full or if she has difficulty moving or if the door is a swinging one that could slam back. You should never allow a door to slam in someone's face. Let the person behind you grab hold of it. And if someone holds a door for you, always say, "Thank you."

Revolving Doors

Turnabout is fair play with revolving doors designed to speed two-way traffic flows through the same small space. However, for a revolving door to function effectively, those entering and leaving must adopt the same pace and rhythm. Getting synchronized requires courteous cooperation. Abrupt stops and sudden changes in speed can be both rude and dangerous.

When you are a host bringing someone in or out of a building with a revolving door, lead the way by going first. You may want to provide directions, such as "I'll meet you at the other side" or "See you at the sidewalk." Push the door, but not too fast. Once you have exited, wait for your party to join you. If more than one person is following you, wait until everyone has come through the revolving door.

Someone who is a slow walker or perhaps fearful about entering a revolving door should wait until most of the other traffic has cleared. He can then proceed at his own pace. Of course, if you happen to arrive immediately after such a person has entered the door, it's polite to either wait until he has exited or to slow your speed rather than pushing him through.

UPS AND DOWNS: ELEVATOR ETIQUETTE

Not so long ago, most elevators had human operators to make sure that the equipment functioned properly. Elevator operators were also transportation moderators, who encouraged people to "Step to the back, please" or announced, "Sixth floor." Today, we rely on elevator riders to politely police themselves.

Rude Riders

Alas, not all elevator riders know or practice courteous behavior. On the following list, mark an *(I)* for *impolite* practices and *(P)* for *polite* behaviors:

_____   1. Pushing all of the up (or down) buttons for all the elevators arriving in a corridor.

_____   2. Putting your hand on the rubber strip to hold the door so people can exit or enter.

_____   3. Pushing the button for someone else's floor at his or her request.

_____   4. Stating "This elevator is full. Please wait for the next one."

_____   5. Entering the elevator as soon as the door opens, before the people inside have exited.

———   **6.** Moving to the back or side to make room for others.

The more crowded and the slower the elevators are, the greater the need for courteous behavior. Polite riders adopt a group mentality, acknowledging that the elevator is not their own personal conveyance. This approach is actually more efficient: It speeds everyone on his or her way. For instance, if you hog the space by standing in the middle of the elevator in hopes of making a quick exit, others are forced to maneuver around you. This slows up everyone, including you.

A host should walk a departing visitor to the elevator and wait with him until it arrives. A host who is accompanying the visitor to another floor should hold the elevator door and allow the guest to enter the elevator first. When leaving, depending on where the host is in the elevator, she should exit and hold the door for her guest while directing him where to go next.

4

If... Then...

Finish each sentence by matching it with the appropriate ending.

If ...	Then ...
——— **1.** The elevator stops at a floor that isn't yours.	**A.** Get out, holding the door so you aren't left behind.
——— **2.** You are in the front of a very crowded elevator and someone behind you needs to leave.	**B.** Move to allow people in and out.
	C. Introduce everyone.
——— **3.** You are in the back of a crowded elevator.	**D.** Say hello and exchange pleasantries.
——— **4.** Someone you recognize gets on the elevator.	**E.** Speak up when you are about to reach your floor.
——— **5.** Someone you know joins you and a colleague on the elevator.	

Answers: 1-B, 2-A, 3-E, 4-D, 5-C

Answers: 1-I, 2-P, 3-P, 4-P, 5-I, 6-P

TAXICAB COURTESY

The true test of your good manners may come late one cold and rainy Friday afternoon when you—along with what seems to be half the entire city—try to hail a cab to get you home in time for dinner. Fatigue and discomfort may conspire to replace your basic graciousness with whatever aggressiveness it takes to get you on your way. In some big cities, it's the survival of the fastest—whoever makes it to the cab door first gets the ride. Even so, proper etiquette insists that you never elbow anyone aside.

■ Curbside Courtesy

Test your knowledge of curbside courtesy with this true-false test. The answers are on page 45.

T F   **1.** In some locations, you must call ahead rather than hail a cab on the street.

T F   **2.** To hail a cab, step into the street, raise your arm, and whistle.

T F   **3.** Hailing taxis isn't part of the hotel doorman's job description.

T F   **4.** An appropriate tip for a doorman who helps you get a cab is $1, more if he helps you load luggage.

T F   **5.** When two people are seeking a cab at the same location, the one who arrived first gets the first cab.

T F   **6.** When a man and a woman are seeking a cab at the same location, the man should always let the woman get the first cab.

T F   **7.** In some cities, people may share a cab and the costs, even if they are going to different destinations.

T F   **8.** It's rude for a passenger not to initiate a conversation with the cab driver.

T F   **9.** If the cab driver gets stuck in a traffic jam, you should suggest that he or she turn off the meter.

T F   **10.** An appropriate tip for your cab driver is 15 percent of your fare.

SENSIBLE SEATING

Once you arrive at your meeting, you probably want to sit down and get on with business. However, it's rude and reckless to pull up a seat before being invited to do so. You don't want to take someone else's seat by mistake. What's more, the meeting may not be in the room that you first enter.

The host should indicate where the visitor should sit, and the visitor should wait for the host to do so before sitting down. If the host fails to indicate a chair (perhaps out of forgetfulness), it's a good idea to inquire before sitting down. The visitor puts a briefcase or purse on the floor, not the desk that is the host's territory.

When sitting, make sure that you sit up straight rather than slouching. Don't fidget, shift in your seat, or tap your feet. Any of these can indicate impatience. If you cross your legs, do so at the ankles rather than the knees.

The host should sit next to the visitor if possible. If the office is too small for side-by-side seating, the host should place a chair beside her desk. The desk should not be a physical barrier between the host and visitor.

As a visitor, you should move the chair only if your host gives permission or invites you to do so. If you do move the chair, replace it in its original position when you leave. If you need to get closer than the chair allows, try leaning closer, or stand up—temporarily—so that you can see the document you are discussing.

PHYSICAL DISTANCE: REASONABLE PROXIMITY

In our U.S. business environment, invading someone's space may be intimidating or too intimate. When someone comes very near, we may reflexively brace for either a personal expression of affection or for a physical assault.

Similarly, we use body language to communicate psychological distance from someone. We describe someone who is aloof as *standoffish*. When people wish to communicate displeasure, they may literally *stand back* from the object of their disdain.

In a business setting, you should rarely, if ever, touch a person. That is an intimacy subject to misinterpretation, even if you think it is being done in a playful, friendly, or even comforting manner. People have vastly different tolerances for physical contact, based on their upbringing, past experiences, and personal notions of what is proper. When in doubt, don't.

Keeping an appropriate distance can help to keep your professional reputation intact. A comfortable distance for people communicating in the workplace is approximately three feet, or about an arm's length away.

Describe a time when someone at work made you feel uncomfortable by getting too close to you: _____
_____
_____

Describe a time when someone at work made you feel uncomfortable by staying too far away from you: _____
_____
_____

4

TERRITORIAL TACTICS

The way we approach people and move while we are communicating is a nonverbal language, a system of subtle signals that conveys our attitudes and professionalism. Just as we wouldn't want to actually step on anyone's toes, we don't want to symbolically do so either. Treating others with appropriate graciousness works much like a revolving door: The momentum of polite behavior helps you and those around you, even when you're going in different directions.

Answers to true-false quiz on page 42:

1–True. In some locations, you must call ahead rather than hailing a cab on the street. When traveling to a new city or location, you should always check in advance.

2–False. To hail a cab, lean toward the street, but do not step into it—that could be dangerous. You can raise your hand, but in most circumstances, you don't need to gesture wildly or whistle loudly.

3–False. Hailing taxis is indeed part of the hotel doorman's job description. Proper etiquette requires that you allow the hotel staff to perform this service rather than taking it upon yourself.

4–True. An appropriate tip for a doorman who helps you get a cab is $1 and more if he helps you load luggage.

5–True. When two people are seeking a cab at the same location, the one who arrived first gets the first cab.

6–False. When a man and a woman are seeking a cab at the same location, the man is not obligated to let the woman get the first cab. Either party can yield to the other person. Although it's particularly gracious to do so if the other person has a pressing commitment and you do not, yielding is an option, not a requirement.

7–True. In some cities, such as Washington, D.C., people may share a cab and the costs, even if they are going to different destinations.

8–False. It's not rude if a passenger fails to initiate a conversation with the cab driver, although it is of course gracious to respond, briefly, if the driver makes a comment. When traffic is congested and you are in a hurry, you do not want to distract the driver with idle chatter. If you need to review papers on the way to a meeting, you can indicate this to the driver, who should respect your need for silence.

9–False. If the cab gets stuck in a traffic jam, you should not suggest that the driver turn off the meter because drivers are reimbursed partly for time as well as for mileage. You should know in advance how the fare is calculated. (Some fares are a flat rate, some are per person, and some are calculated by meter.) You also should make sure that you have enough money to cover unexpected contingencies.

10–True. An appropriate tip is 15 percent of your fare. Have the tip ready, along with the fare, so that you can make a quick exit.

Chapter Checkpoints

✓ Whoever gets to a door first opens it. At revolving doors, match your pace and rhythm to those of others.

✓ A guest enters an elevator before the host. The host can leave first, holding the door for the guest.

✓ When two people are seeking a cab at the same location, the one who arrived first gets the first cab.

✓ A guest should wait to sit down until invited to do so by a host.

✓ A comfortable distance for people communicating in business is approximately three feet apart.

5 | Office Equipment Etiquette

This chapter will help you to:

- Use technology with courtesy.
- Improve your telephone manners.
- Politely share office equipment, including copiers, fax machines, and coffee pots.

After a highly successful presentation, Jenna Glass left her client's office feeling confident and encouraged. She wasn't very far down the street, however, when her car phone began ringing. Very quickly, her good humor began to evaporate.

As Jenna navigated her way through traffic, the ringing of the phone was at first an inconvenience and then a major annoyance. No one had ever called her before. She had used the car phone only to place outgoing calls. While struggling to drive safely, she pushed each button, shouting "Hello? Hello?" Her frustration mounted when she realized she had pushed all the buttons and still was not connected with anyone.

As the traffic congestion increased, Jenna's mind raced. Who could be calling her? Her secretary? No, her secretary knew she would be back after the presentation. Her manager? Had he already heard something that contradicted her impression of a positive reception? Her family? Could there have been an emergency? She felt both frantic and inept.

Not until Jenna reached her office 45 minutes later was she able to find out the reason for the call. The people at her presentation had been trying to reach her—to let her know that she had left her purse behind! ■

PLUGGED-IN POLITENESS

We often have a love-hate relationship with technology. Modern conveniences are both essential business tools and impersonal intrusions on our time. Who hasn't been annoyed when interrupted by an unimportant telephone call or by a fax that had to be retransmitted? Or, we might race to the photocopier minutes before a key meeting to copy an important report and push the button for 25 copies—only to discover that the last person to use the machine let the paper run out or left the copier set for legal-sized documents! Sometimes, we might even wish someone would invent the courtesy microchip—a silicon device that would automatically program our equipment for gracious operation.

The problem, of course, lies not with the equipment but with the people who use it. Devices that enable us to do our jobs faster, across greater distances, and with less human contact do not eliminate the need for polite people. If anything, the nature of inanimate objects *increases* the need for diplomatic, cordial human contact. Much as we might like to blame a machine when we're treated rudely, we know that a person is really responsible.

The impact of equipment snafus on business can be significant. Would you continue to do business with someone who treated you rudely—perhaps by failing to return your phone calls? As a supervisor, would you give a positive evaluation to an employee who caused friction among the staff by failing to share time on the computer? Would you trust a colleague who intercepted your faxes?

■ Manners for Machines

Human creativity keeps coming up with new ways to demonstrate poor manners through office equipment. In what ways have you or someone you know been offended by the use or misuse of the following equipment?

Telephone: _____

_____

Voice mail: _____

_____

Fax machine: _____

_____

Copier: _____

_____

Computer: _____

_____

Coffee machine: _____

_____

TELEPHONE TECHNIQUES

Your business has two entrances—the front door and the telephone. We often judge the competence and courtesy of a business operation by the way someone answers the telephone.

Appropriate Telephone Answers

Even if you are very busy or in the midst of a problem when the phone rings, you need to sound professional, pleased to hear from the caller, and ready to deal with the caller's concerns. Because the phone must be answered even though the timing is inconvenient, avoid losing business by putting on a convincing act.

Answer your phone promptly and courteously. Let it ring at least once and pick it up within three rings. In a clear, pleasant voice, identify both yourself and your company.

▉ The Number You Have Reached

Record what you usually say when you answer your phone: _____
_____

Now, compare your answer against this list:

Y N   Does your answer include a greeting, such as "Hello"?

Y N   Does it include your full name, rather than just your first name (which is too informal) or just your last name (which can sound too abrupt)?

Y N   Does it include a verb—as in "This *is* Debra Elliot" or "Debra Elliot *speaking*"?

Y N   Especially if you share an extension, does your answer include your department's name?

Y N   Especially if you regularly receive outside calls, does your answer include your company's name?

Y N   Is it less than 10 words long, so that the caller doesn't get worn out listening to it?

The more *yes* answers you marked, the more polite your usual telephone answer is.

Is the Manager In?

You're either in or out, available or not. If your phone is answered by a secretary, don't base your availability to talk on the identity of the caller.

While the caller should state his or her name at the beginning of the call, it's just not gracious to take only calls from certain people. It's far more appropriate for the secretary simply to say, "I'll put you through. May I tell her who's calling?" or "Who shall I say is calling?" If the secretary says, "Who shall I say is calling?" and follows up the answer with, "He's not available," the caller may wonder if the secretary is being honest.

Similarly, callers are not favorably impressed if they are put through the third degree before they are allowed to talk with you. A secretary may screen calls by saying, "Does he know what this call is in reference to?" or "Can I tell her what this is about?" However, it can frustrate, and even infuriate, the caller to have to go through the same story twice, when once is all that is required. No one wants to waste time in this way.

Returning Calls

You should return telephone calls within 24 hours, if not sooner. If the person isn't there, make sure you leave a message. When you are unable to help the caller, it's far more considerate to let him know that than to leave him hanging. This also allows him to move on and look elsewhere.

When you are gone, make sure your co-workers have accurate information about when you will be back so that repeat callers don't get several different versions of the best time to reach you: "She's expected in any time now," "She'll be in this afternoon," "She's on vacation all week."

Sound Check

Your speech on the telephone conveys your professionalism—or lack of it. Your word usage, tone of voice, even whether there are background noises all give your caller information that could affect the overall image of your business.

To improve the impression you make:

- Speak slowly and distinctly.

- Don't shout or raise your voice.
- Pay attention to your diction and grammar.
- Don't chew gum or eat while talking or listening on the phone.
- Be enthusiastic. Smile, or sound as if you're smiling.
- If you must sneeze or cough, turn your head, cover your mouth or the mouthpiece, and say, "Excuse me."
- Reduce distracting background noise, including interference on the line. If need be, switch to another location or call back.

Transferring Calls and Handling Holds

Putting people on hold and making telephone transfers are necessary evils. To minimize frustrations for the caller, put people on hold or transfer calls only when necessary. Limit the amount of time involved whenever possible, and keep in close contact with the caller throughout the process.

Give the person a choice before putting her on hold. Say, "May I please put you on hold?" Pause and wait for a response.

When you return to the call, thank the caller for holding.

If you put someone on hold, get back every 20 to 30 seconds or so to check if the person is still there. Let the person know what is happening: "It will take me a couple of minutes to gather the data. I can put you back on hold or call you in a few minutes."

Consider transferring the person to an appropriate party rather than trying to handle the call yourself while the person is on hold. This can save the caller money, especially if he's calling long distance. Before making the transfer, give the person the new extension, in case you are accidentally disconnected.

Briefly explain the situation to the person you are transferring the caller to, so you can spare the caller from having to explain again. Knowing that a call is being transferred is useful. You can anticipate that the caller's frustration level may be higher than usual and avoid elevating it further.

10 Tips for Placing Polite Calls

When you are placing the call, remember that it might not be a convenient time for the listener to talk. Accordingly, avoid anything that is inconsiderate of or squanders the other person's time. You can demonstrate courtesy in several ways.

1. *Apologize if you dial a wrong number.* Don't just hang up; it's rude. Using call-tracing technology, the recipient could trace the call back to you, which reflects badly on you and your company. Before hanging up, ask the recipient if you reached the number you planned to dial. You may need to look up the number again. Be sure you don't redial the wrong party a second time. Also, remember to say goodbye.

2. *Identify yourself clearly.* If a secretary answers, say, "Hello, this is Hope Simmons of ABC Demographics. Is Mr. Morgan available?" Identify yourself again to the client or customer when you are connected.

Never assume that you can skip identifying yourself when calling someone you call regularly. In a business setting, that presumes an intimacy and a familiarity with your voice that usually just doesn't exist. It's rude to leave the person guessing for part of the conversation or momentarily distracted while trying to figure out who's calling.

If you identify yourself only as Hope, you may be setting yourself up for confusion. (Is it Hope in finance or Hope in Personnel?) Even if you have an unusual name, it's best to use both your first and last names. You can think of this as a form of personal marketing. It helps reinforce your name so that others are better able to address you and introduce you.

3. *Ask if this is a good time to talk.* "Dropping in" unexpectedly by telephone can be as rude as doing so in person. In some companies, first-thing-in-the-morning calls are best, while in other organizations, employees may have more leisure for discussions at day's end.

Say something like, "Larry, I need to talk about the distribution plan. It will take about 15 minutes. Is this a convenient time?"

5

4. *If leaving a message asking someone to call you back, provide your phone number instead of saying, "He has it."* This saves your party from having to look up your number. Provide information on the best time to reach you, especially if you are going to be out of the office.

5. *If someone is going to be listening to your end of the conversation, especially if one of you is on a speaker phone, let the person on the phone know at the beginning.* You can say, "Brenda, Jason's here in the office with me to answer any questions regarding the production side."

6. *Be organized.* Send or fax materials beforehand to save time while talking. Think out in advance what you want to say. Divide your conversation into segments and allow appropriate pauses so that the listener can respond. Have paper and pen available so you can take notes as you talk.

7. *Remember that the first call takes priority.* Unless the head of the company is calling from Europe, try to take a message rather than cut off your original call.

8. *Deal with distractions.* Avoid side conversations with someone else in the room. If you must stop your conversation, let the person on the line know. Say something like, "Please excuse me for just a minute."

If someone arrives in your office, she should leave when she sees you're on the phone. If she doesn't, you can pause, say "Excuse me," to the listener, and then say politely and firmly to the visitor, "I'll be happy to talk when I'm through with this call."

9. *Pay attention to your language.* Call the person by name with the correct title. Be careful about using "you" statements such as "you forgot" or "you should." Instead, put your comments in the form of a question: "Did you send me the report we discussed?" Use verbal prompts—"I see" or "I understand"—to encourage the speaker. Be positive when responding to and making requests: "I'd be happy to take care of that."

10. *Close the conversation.* Summarize what you'll do next. Include a polite acknowledgment, such as "It's been nice talking to you" or "Thank you for calling." Hang up gracefully and gently.

Considerations for Car Phones

Car phones should be used only when absolutely necessary because a call can be distracting, and even dangerous, to the driver. Also, cars aren't the best locations to talk. Unless the driver is parked or stopped in traffic, he cannot give full attention to the conversation.

If you do use a car phone:

- Preprogram the numbers you call regularly.
- Tell the other person that you're on your car phone. In case you get cut off or fade in and out, the listener knows why.
- Plan the call ahead of time.
- Don't try to take notes while you're driving. Instead, pull over at your first opportunity or use a dictation device.
- Speak loudly and clearly, and try to reduce background noise as much as possible. Turn off your radio, roll up the windows, turn down the air conditioner, and so on.
- Anticipate your route. Don't start a call a mile before you reach a tunnel, bridge, tollbooth, or any other obstacle that might interfere with reception.
- Before you call someone on her car phone, make sure it's OK with that person.

5

MANAGING VOICE MAIL AND ANSWERING MACHINE MESSAGES

Answering machines and voice mail are conveniences that allow you to always answer your phone. They help both the caller, who can fulfill at least part of the purpose of the call, and the recipient, who isn't dragged into conversations when it isn't convenient. Like any other messages, messages left on a machine or voice mail should be returned within 24 hours.

Don't use an answering machine as a screening device by picking up only selected calls. It's much more polite to wait 10 minutes and call the person back than to pick up the phone after listening to the message.

5

Tip

This Is a Recording

When creating the message that your callers will hear, be sure you can answer *yes* to the following questions:

- *Did I identify myself with my full name?*
- *Is my message short and to the point?* Did I remind the caller to leave his or her affiliation, phone number, and a brief message?
- *Was I specific about how my system works?* Did I let people know if there is a time limit for their messages? Did I mention that there is more than one beep so they should wait for the long tone? If it's possible for them to press a code and speak to a secretary, did I say so?
- *Did I tell people when I will return or check my messages, so they know about when to expect my return call?* "I'll be back after three" is better than "I'll be in this afternoon."
- *If necessary, did I remember to turn on the machine when I stepped out?*

Leaving Messages

If you had a reason to make a phone call, you have reason enough to leave a message. Some tips on leaving messages:

- Listen to make sure you reached the person you dialed.
- Speak slowly and clearly, starting with your name and phone number.

- Make sure the messages you leave are intended for semipublic consumption. Voice mail may be heard by someone other than the person you called.
- If the person's machine seems to be malfunctioning, let him know that in your message.
- Repeat your name and phone number at the end.
- Remember to exit the system if necessary, not just hang up.
- If someone for whom you left a message doesn't call back within a reasonable time, assume the machine is at fault and try again.

POLITE PROTOCOL FOR SHARED EQUIPMENT

5

Much as we like to think of the equipment at work as ours, we know it really isn't. We get to borrow it and may even have relatively exclusive rights to use it, but we, of course, don't own it—the company does. When others need to use the same equipment, we need to apply basic principles of courtesy and decency so that the system works smoothly. While each type of equipment has its own set of rules, there are some guiding principles.

Tip ─────────────────────────────

Courtesy for Shared Equipment

Learn how to use the equipment properly. If you guess wrong, you may inconvenience others.

Take turns.

Clean up your mess before leaving the area.

If it's empty, fill it.

If it breaks, fix it or get it fixed.

Don't take, borrow, or snoop through what isn't yours.

Leave equipment ready for the next user.

5

FAX MACHINE FINESSE

People today think of fax machines as a speedy form of mail; in reality, they're quite different. Sending a letter doesn't prevent someone from receiving other mail at the same time, and the recipient can throw the letter away unopened.

For these reasons, don't send unsolicited faxes. They can tie up someone's machine, waste paper, *and* reveal poor manners and lack of consideration. You also might need the recipient's permission to send the fax because some machines are turned on only at stipulated times. In a large

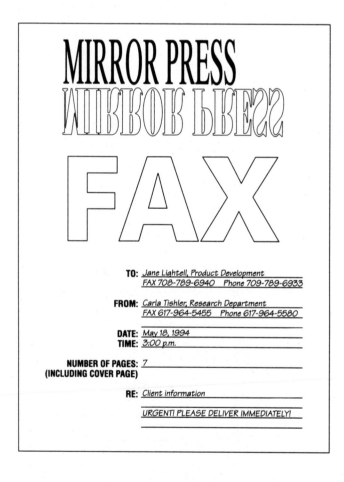

MIRROR PRESS

FAX

TO: _Jane Lightell, Product Development_
FAX 708-789-6940   Phone 709-789-6933

FROM: _Carla Tishler, Research Department_
FAX 617-964-5455   Phone 617-964-5580

DATE: _May 18, 1994_
TIME: _3:00 p.m._

NUMBER OF PAGES: _7_
(INCLUDING COVER PAGE)

RE: _Client information_

URGENT! PLEASE DELIVER IMMEDIATELY!

corporation, the fax printer may not be near the recipient, so she needs to know when to be on the lookout for what you're sending.

Reasonable Facsimiles

There are many good reasons to think about how and why to fax materials as well as which materials to fax. Match each of the following appropriate behaviors with the rationale that supports it. Some of the reasons support more than one behavior.

5

_____ 1. Don't fax restricted-access materials without advance permission.

_____ 2. Be creative about sending times—use early morning or lunchtime.

_____ 3. Make sure your cover sheet includes the to and from fax and phone numbers, the recipient's and sender's names and departments, the number of pages in the fax, the time and date sent, and any messages, including whether delivery is urgent.

_____ 4. Follow company rules about personal use of the fax to order lunch or concert tickets, for instance.

_____ 5. When sending a fax, call to let the other person know when to expect it.

_____ 6. Don't fax items required for permanent records or items that require actual signatures.

_____ 7. If you find a received fax, put it in the recipient's mail box and don't read beyond the cover sheet.

_____ 8. Don't change the fax's programming or automatic dial numbers unless you have permission.

A. This helps the fax get to the recipient quickly.

B. The fax machine is less likely to be tied up, and you could save your company money.

C. The fax is first and foremost a tool for business.

D. The fax has aspects of private communication and should be treated as such.

E. Fax printing does not last over time. The document is not an original.

F. The fax is a community communications device. Nothing should be changed at whim.

Answers: 1–D, 2–B, 3–A, 4–C, 5–A, 6–E, 7–D, 8–F

5

COPIER COURTESY

Most courtesy conflicts over copiers fall into two categories: large jobs or care and feeding.

Large jobs.   The person with the fewest number of copies to make gets priority. Let someone interrupt your large project if the person has only one or two sheets to copy. If two people arrive at the same time, let the person with fewer copies go first. If you arrive when a large job is in process, you can say, "Do you mind if I interrupt? I have just two copies to make." Be sure to check the paper supply after completing a large copy job, and refill the copier if necessary. Don't use the machine to make large numbers of personal copies unless you supply your own paper and run copies during off-hours, provided that's an acceptable practice in your office.

Care and feeding.   Do any necessary maintenance, such as resupplying toner or fixing paper jams, yourself. Don't leave problems for the next person. Always remember to reset the machine after using it—usually to one copy, 8½-by-11-inch size. Make sure that you take your original with you!

APPROPRIATE COMPUTER ACCESS

It's your responsibility to know how to use the company computer. If you need to ask for help or instructions after your initial training period, do so at a time that's convenient for the person helping you. Here are more tips regarding computer courtesy:

- Try to coordinate projects on the computer so everyone knows in advance when the equipment is available. Be realistic about how much time you need. Respect office guidelines and timelines, and defer to projects with higher priority.
- Refill the paper supply in the printer, add toner, replenish the available supply of blank disks, and call the appropriate person when repairs are needed.

- Do not change the programming to suit your individual needs.
- Do not use someone else's disks or sign-on password without receiving permission.
- Do not read confidential plans, reports, or files.
- Remember to keep the area clean and to take all your papers with you when you leave.

A few cautions about fun and games: It's courteous and smart to respect corporate rules about playing computer games on company time. Taking up memory needed for other projects is just plain greedy.

RESOLVING SIMMERING FEUDS OVER COFFEE MACHINES

5

Coffee machines don't take care of themselves—someone has to fill, empty, and clean them. If this is not part of someone's job description, the task can be rotated or randomly assigned to whoever arrives first or leaves last.

If you drink from the coffee pot, however, it's your job to help maintain it throughout the day. If you empty the pot, start a new one. If you don't know how to start a new pot, learn how to do so. Wipe up any spills and, as many mothers used to say, keep your mug clean.

Many offices provide regular and decaffeinated coffee, as well as hot water and tea bags. Cream, sugar, sugar substitute, stirrers, and napkins should also be available. If you use the last of any of these supplies, get out refills or alert the appropriate person.

If the system is pay as you go, make sure that you do.

5

THE POWER OF BEING POLITE

The Golden Rule—"Do unto others as you would have them do unto you"—applies in many office situations, from the telephone to shared use of equipment. A polite approach that takes the needs of others into account can reduce office tension and improve morale, thus making business more efficient.

Chapter Checkpoints

✓ The increased use of more impersonal office equipment makes courteous conduct especially important.

✓ Telephone courtesy includes respecting the time of the person at the other end of the line.

✓ When sharing equipment, keep the needs of other users in mind.

6 | Packaging Counts
Professional Presence

This chapter will help you to:

- Improve your grooming routine.
- Develop a work wardrobe that works well for you.

When Edward Alan, a field sales manager for a newspaper, arrived at corporate headquarters for a lunch meeting, he was wearing pink casual slacks, a pink shirt, and a matching tie. As soon as Edward walked in, his manager cornered him and said, "I can't tell you *not* to wear those clothes again, but if I were you, I wouldn't. Those clothes can affect your relationships here. Pink is not our corporate color." ∎

Your professional presence—the way you come across to others—is created by the way you dress and groom yourself. An appropriate appearance demonstrates respect for yourself, others, and the situation.

To look your best, you need to pay attention to the details of your appearance. Often, others judge you by how well groomed you are and by whether your clothing makes you look professional. Appropriate, attractive packaging can make the difference in how others perceive you.

Imagine that you are eating lunch in the food court of a shopping mall near an office complex. Based only on how the following people are described, write down any assumptions you would make about them. Describe the jobs you think they would have. Indicate which of them you would trust with an important project.

Well-groomed man wearing bold plaid sports coat and trousers:

_____

_____

Woman with long hair, dressed in tight-fitting, low-cut dress and spike heels: _____

_____

Woman with long hair pulled back from her face, dressed in dark suit and pumps: _____

_____

Well-groomed man wearing jeans, a flannel shirt and tinted glasses:

_____

_____

Man with stylishly cut hair, dressed in a suit with a tie:

_____

_____

Your perceptions of these people are based on your own background and experiences. The point is that we are always making judgments about the people we see, based on the way they look. Also, we are always sending out nonverbal signals by our own choice of wardrobe and by the way we groom ourselves.

ELIMINATING GROOMING GAFFES

Grooming—refining the basic daily habits that give you a neat and tidy appearance—is an essential part of your professional presence. You can be exceptionally well dressed but still make a bad impression because of your grooming. Picture a woman with runs in her stockings, lingerie showing, and lipstick on her teeth, or a man with perspiration stains in the armpits of his shirt, food stains on his tie, and dandruff. When grooming is not appropriate, it can be distracting to others and detracts from your professional reputation. However, when you are well groomed, your over-all image is enhanced.

Describe a grooming gaffe you've noticed that someone at work often commits: _____

_____

In what ways is someone at work always well groomed? _____

_____

_____

■ Grooming Strengths and Weaknesses

Look in the mirror, and then check any of the following items that apply to you. Be honest. Does your assessment reflect how others see you?

6

_____   Hair is trimmed and well styled.

_____   Hair is clean and free of dandruff.

_____   Makeup is well designed and appropriately applied.

_____   Face is clean-shaven, no five o'clock shadow.

_____   Nose and ear hairs are trimmed.

_____   Fingernails are clean or polished.

_____   Amount of perfume or cologne is restrained.

_____   Teeth are polished.

_____   Breath is fresh.

_____   Glasses fit well and are clean.

_____   Posture is good—shoulders back, head up.

From time to time, of course, we all commit grooming gaffes. These are not limited to basic body maintenance but can extend to clothing and other appearance essentials. Mark the following list *(E)* for mishaps that you have *experienced*, *(O)* for mishaps you've *observed*, and *(H)* for mis-haps you've *heard* about from others:

——— Food-stained clothing.

——— Fly-away hair, hairpiece, or wig.

——— Slip or underwear showing.

——— Stockings or socks that don't match each other or clothing.

——— A run, snag, or sag in hosiery. Wrong jacket with suit.

——— Hem unraveled.

——— Frayed collar or cuffs.

——— Wrinkled clothing.

——— Fly unzipped.

——— Button missing or unbuttoned.

——— Overdone makeup.

——— Too much jewelry.

——— Shoes need polishing.

——— Shoes with worn heels.

It pays to check the mirror periodically. Your daily routine should allow time for inspection before you leave home as well as during breaks and after meals.

ESTABLISHING AN IMPRESSIVE IMAGE

You want people to focus on your professional abilities—not your physical attributes, no matter how attractive you might be. Calling attention to your body, whether positively or negatively, decreases the significance of your skills, accomplishments, and contributions.

Describe a situation in which a person's clothing detracted from appreciation of his or her work skills: _____

_____

_____

CLOTHING SELECTION CRITERIA

Many factors go into determining whether an outfit is appropriate for your work environment. While clothing is a personal expression, it also is a nonverbal statement of your willingness to be a team player. What's more, what's suitable in one part of the country or in one industry may be inappropriate in another. Ask yourself the following list of questions when purchasing a new work outfit. If you can't answer *yes* to most of them, select another outfit.

Y N **1.** Is the outfit appropriate for the job and for my position?

Y N **2.** Does it fit in with what other people at my company wear?

Y N **3.** Does it fit in with what other people in this region of the country wear?

Y N **4.** Is this the correct season for this outfit?

Y N **5.** While wearing this outfit, can I comfortably do whatever physical tasks my job requires, such as writing on a flip chart or demonstrating equipment?

Y N **6.** Is it suitable for the particular situation where I intend to wear it (a meeting with an important client, Saturday afternoon inventory review)?

Y N **7.** Does it fit me?

Y N **8.** Can I sit down without the buttons pulling in front?

Y N **9.** Does it look as if it fits when viewed from the front, back, and side?

Y N **10.** Does it look good?

Y N **11.** Is this an attractive color on me?

Y N **12.** Will I wear it often?

Y N **13.** If it is a shirt or a blouse, will it go with other items in my wardrobe?

Y N **14.** Does it send a professional message?

6

Y N   **15.** Would I feel confident if I wore it on the same day my rival for the next promotion wore his or her most professional-looking outfit—and we met with the head of personnel?

Y N   **16.** Do I like it?

WARDROBE SAVVY

To look professional, you need to do more than choose the right clothing. You must make sure that it fits and that you wear it correctly. Differences in fabric, color, and styling all have an impact on the appropriateness of an outfit.

Test your knowledge of clothing considerations with this true-false quiz. The answers can be found on page 77.

T F   **1.** You can leave a double-breasted jacket unbuttoned.

T F   **2.** The tip of a man's tie should extend to the middle of his belt.

T F   **3.** Linen is a good fabric choice for suits because it is lightweight and can be worn almost year-round.

T F   **4.** Men's dress shirts should always be long-sleeved, even in summer, so that the cuffs show about a half inch below the jacket.

T F   **5.** A coat-style dress (a tailored dress with buttons all the way down the front) is just as powerful a look as a woman's business suit.

T F   **6.** The best fabric choice for both men's shirts and women's blouses is 100 percent cotton.

T F   **7.** A man's suit jacket should be long enough to cover the buttocks.

T F   **8.** Good colors for a woman's hosiery include nude, taupe, or one shade darker than her skin tone.

T   F   **9.** Power colors recommended for suits are navy, gray, charcoal, and black; brown should be avoided.

T   F   **10.** The color of a man's tie should contrast with the color of his jacket.

T   F   **11.** Tinted or photogray glasses are good choices, because you don't have to carry two pairs.

T   F   **12.** Tasseled loafers are universally acceptable choices for men's footwear.

T   F   **13.** The color of a woman's shoes should be the color of her dress or skirt hemline or darker.

T   F   **14.** A man's belt should match his shoes.

T   F   **15.** Men should wear black shoes with gray, navy, or black suits.

T   F   **16.** To less formal events, such as corporate-sponsored picnics or pool parties, women can wear sandals, shorts, or bikini bathing suits.

T   F   **17.** On dress down days at the office, it's OK for men to wear tattered jeans.

T   F   **18.** It's OK for women to wear sexy outfits to a company cocktail party.

The Cost of Clothing

A professional wardrobe is an investment. If you buy the most expensive merchandise that you can reasonably afford, you will probably get your money's worth. To determine the actual cost of an outfit, use this formula:

$$\frac{\text{Cost}}{\substack{\text{Total number} \\ \text{of wearings}}} = \text{Cost per wearing}$$

Calculate the cost of each of these outfits to determine which is the best buy:

A $250 wool gabardine navy suit, worn 10 months of the year, once a week, for four years:

_____ wearings per month × _____ months × _____ years = wearings

_____(cost)   = $_____ cost per
(number of wearings)   wearing

A $100 dress, worn nine months of the year, once a month, for two years:

_____ wearings per month × _____ months × _____ years = wearings

_____(cost)   = $_____ cost per
(number of wearings)   wearing

A $300 coat, worn five months of the year, five times a week, for three years:

_____ wearings per month × _____ months × _____ years = wearings

_____(cost)   = $_____ cost per
(number of wearings)   wearing

A $150 coat, worn four months of the year, twice a week, for two years:

_____ wearings per month × _____ months × _____ years = wearings

_____(cost)   = $_____ cost per
(number of wearings)   wearing

When buying a new outfit, you can use this same formula to determine whether the outfit is a good value. Estimate the number of times you expect to wear it, and divide that number into the cost.

_____ expected wearings per month × _____ months × _____ years = _____ expected total wearings

_____(cost)   = $_____ cost per
(number of expected   wearing
total wearings)

You also can monitor how often you actually wear the new outfit compared to the number of times you thought you would wear it. If you wear it less, ask yourself why. If you wear it more, you've probably made a good selection.

SAMPLE WARDROBES

On the following page are some basic wardrobes to give you a starting point for assessing your own wardrobe. Your skin and hair coloring may influence the final color choice of items.

■ What to Buy

Take inventory of your business wardrobe, thinking about what you might need to achieve a more professional look. List what you need to buy to complete your wardrobe:

_____   _____
_____   _____
_____   _____
_____   _____

A SMART STYLE

When we go to work, we are getting ready to perform roles, much like actors or actresses preparing to step onto the stage. How we look helps determine how our audience—composed of co-workers and supervisors—perceives us, although, of course, our performance matters, too! Nevertheless, when we look the part as professionals, our appearance contributes to, rather than detracts from, our overall image. What's more, just as a performer's makeup and costume can help her make the transition to the character being portrayed, appropriate grooming and attire can make us *feel*, as well as look, competent and confident.

6

6

Women's Basic Business Wardrobe

Black or gray suit

Navy suit

Three coordinating jackets and skirts

Two-piece dress

Five solid-color blouses

Two pastel or print blouses

Gold, silver, and good costume earrings, necklace, bracelet, pin, and a good-quality watch

Scarf that picks up colors from a suit (optional)

Pair of black pumps

Pair of navy or taupe pumps

Black leather bag

Black belt and navy belt

Black, brown, or burgundy briefcase

All-weather coat

Men's Basic Business Wardrobe

One navy suit

One charcoal gray suit

Medium blue or gray suit

Two or three pinstriped or other subtle pattern suits

Six white cotton shirts, long-sleeved

Blue or pin-striped shirt

All-weather coat

Five to eight solid, striped, or patterned silk ties

Leather briefcase

Two black leather belts

One pair black lace-up shoes

One pair black slip-on shoes

One good-quality watch

Answers to true-false quiz on pages 72–73:

1-False. A double-breasted jacket should always be buttoned, including the inside button.

2-True. The tip of a man's tie should extend to the middle of his belt. It should be no shorter than the top of the belt.

3-False. Linen is not a good fabric choice for suits because it wrinkles easily. Purchase linen only if it is blended with such fabrics as polyester, rayon, or acrylic.

4-True. Men's dress shirts should always be long-sleeved, even in summer, so that the cuffs show about half an inch below the jacket. Fortunately for those who work in hot climates, office air conditioning is now standard!

5-False. A coat-style dress (a tailored dress with buttons all the way down the front) is not as powerful-looking as a woman's business suit, but it is very appropriate for certain situations.

6-False. The best fabric choice for men's shirts is 100 percent cotton, but for women, silk is a better choice, even though it can be expensive and often needs to be dry-cleaned. Cotton is an acceptable choice, provided it is starched and carefully pressed.

7-True. A man's suit jacket should be long enough to cover the buttocks.

8-True. Good colors for a woman's hosiery include nude, taupe, or one shade darker than her skin tone. Pale gray and bone also are good neutral colors.

9-True. Power colors recommended for men's suits are navy, gray, charcoal, and black; brown should be avoided. You need to be careful with black, which can be intimidating.

10-True. The color of a man's tie should contrast with the color of his jacket.

11-False. Tinted or photogray glasses are not good choices, because others can't see the wearer's eyes. Photogray glasses also don't usually lighten up enough indoors. Carry a pair of sunglasses if you need them.

12-False. Tasseled loafers are less conservative than leather lace-up shoes and may be considered inappropriate in some industries.

13-True. The color of a woman's shoes should be the color of her dress or skirt hemline or darker.

14-True. A man's belt should match his shoes.

15-True. Men should wear black shoes with gray, navy, or black suits.

16-False. To less formal events, women can wear sandals or sneakers. However, it is not appropriate to wear a bikini.

17-False. In corporate environments, it would not be OK for men to wear tattered jeans to the office even on dress down days. In some environments, clean, well-pressed jeans may be acceptable. Know your work situation. Slacks and chinos are always acceptable.

18-False. Women should not wear sexy outfits to a company cocktail party. The party is still business.

6

Chapter Checkpoints

✓ Appropriate grooming can give you professional polish. Inappropriate grooming is distracting.

✓ Your work wardrobe should fit and flatter you, while sending a professional message.

✓ What's appropriate for your office depends on the type of job you do, the area of the country in which you live, the climate, and the specific situation for which you are dressing.

✓ Quality clothing is less expensive in the long run than trendy clothing, because the cost per number of wearings is less.

7 | The Social Niceties

Gift-Giving and Party Performances

This chapter will help you to: ────────

- Present appropriate business gifts.
- Understand how to behave when entertaining clients or attending business social events outside the office.
- Act appropriately at office parties.

Two long-time business colleagues had distinctly different ways of handling each other's birthdays. Each year, Faith Naldone sent a birthday card to her associate, Kay Dennison, always selecting a tasteful acknowledgment of that special day in the life of someone she both respected and liked. Kay, however, chose to ignore Faith's birthday, even though she reciprocated Faith's feelings of friendship. This went on for years.

One year, though, Kay did not receive a birthday card from Faith. After mulling over what she might have done to offend her friend and pondering possible explanations, Kay finally asked Faith, "Why didn't you send me a birthday card this year?" Faith explained that she hadn't sent a card because she had never received any in return. That year, on Faith's birthday, she received 20 cards from Kay to make up for all the birthdays Kay had missed. Now, Kay always gets a birthday card from Faith, and Faith always gets a birthday card from Kay. ■

The social niceties aren't part of your official job description, but your ability to handle them with finesse can improve your professional image. If you are the only one who fails to acknowledge your boss's promotion or if you offend clients while playing golf with them or if you dress inappropriately for the company holiday party, you can undermine your professional reputation. When you are professionally competent, social niceties are the polish on your performance.

Describe a time your career, or that of someone you know, was enhanced because of the way a business social situation was handled:

_____

_____

Describe a time your career, or that of someone you know, suffered because of the way a business social situation was handled:

_____

_____

7

GRACIOUS GIFT-GIVING

A business gift can convey many meanings: thank-you for a job well done, congratulations on your promotion, sorry to hear about your brother's death, happy holidays, or best wishes for your retirement. Customs regarding gift-giving vary greatly between companies, and sometimes even between departments.

Before giving someone a business gift, consult the following list. You should be able to answer *yes* to all the questions.

Y   N   Does the situation fit within company and departmental policy regarding gift-giving?

Y   N   Does the situation conform to company and department traditions regarding gift-giving?

Y   N   Is the timing for this particular gift appropriate?

Y   N   Does the gift acknowledge the likes and dislikes of the recipient?

Y   N   Is the cost of the gift appropriate?

Y   N   Is the gift itself appropriate?

The main consideration in deciding whether to give a gift is your own relationship with the recipient. For instance, employees are usually advised not to give gifts to managers because such gift-giving can be seen as currying favor. However, if you work in a small office and are unusually close to your manager, a holiday gift may be appropriate. Similarly, it may be more appropriate for you to contribute to a departmental wedding gift than to provide an individual one if you do not know the person who is getting married very well.

If the situation does not lend itself to a gift, a card may be appropriate. Make sure that the card is tasteful, timely, and appropriately addressed. A congratulations card, a thank-you, or a condolence card should include a handwritten note.

When to Give Gifts

Some circumstances naturally lend themselves to gift-giving. We've listed the most common situations along with comments on the types of relationships in which such gifts are appropriate. On the lines after each category, list your own upcoming situations along with the name of anyone you'd like to honor with a gift.

Familial events—births, weddings, showers, and funerals—involving employees and their families.   Acknowledge the birth of a child to an employee, client, customer, colleague, manager, or manager's spouse. Give a gift or contribute to the group gift for a wedding or baby shower. Send a gift if you attend a wedding. Send flowers or fruit with a card in case of the death of a close relative (parent, sibling, spouse, child) of an employee, manager, colleague, vendor, client, or customer. You also can make a donation to a charity designated by the family of the deceased.

_____

_____

_____

Personal events directly affecting an employee, including a birthday or serious illness. Cards are always appropriate. You can observe a colleague's special birthday—such as a 40th—even if you have ignored the day in other years. A manager may give an employee flowers or a birthday lunch or dinner certificate. An employee usually should not mark the manager's birthday. Send plants that need little care to hospital patients or send cut flowers when patients go home.

_____

_____

_____

Company occasions including promotion, retirement, and special employment anniversaries. Official gifts are provided by the department or the company, such as a gold watch for retirement. Individual cards are appropriate, and many stores now offer an entire line of greeting cards aimed at this market. A gift is sometimes appropriate.

_____

_____

_____

Secretary's Day. Depending on your corporate culture, provide flowers, a special lunch out, or a small gift such as a picture frame for your secretary. If you work with a secretarial pool, coordinate your plans with others, possibly sending a floral arrangement from all of you to each secretary. As a customer, vendor, or client, you may choose to recognize the work of a client's secretary who has been especially helpful.

_____

_____

_____

Thank you. A hostess gift is required every time you are treated to dinner at a co-worker's home. Gifts can include boxed chocolates, packages of teas, party napkins, or flowers that are sent ahead of time or the following day. A business thank-you may be appropriate if someone has done something above and beyond his or her usual duties. For instance, you might acknowledge an employee's extra effort to make an important deadline or thank a client for a number of years of loyal patronage.

_____

_____

_____

Holiday gifts, including seasonal year-end remembrances. Holiday cards are always appropriate, but they should have a general message, such as "season's greetings," since not everyone celebrates religious holidays. Employees generally don't give managers holiday presents, although in some circumstances, gifts may be appropriate.

_____

_____

_____

What to Spend

You want to give something of quality, but a gift doesn't have to be expensive. An item that reflects the taste and desires of the recipient is happily received regardless of the price. Take into account your company policy, your salary, the number of donors for a particular gift, and the number of times gifts are given.

What to Buy

It's especially important that a business gift be suitable for the situation. Avoid gifts with romantic connotations (such as long-stemmed roses) and highly personal gifts (such as clothing) —and be very careful about gag gifts. Food is a generally appreciated gift that can be personalized to the recipient's taste. Use caution when selecting wine or liquor as a gift. Other generally safe gifts include professional presents—items such as a pocket calendar, a letter opener, a book, or bookends.

7

What was the best business gift you ever received? What made it so memorable? _____

_____

_____

What was the best business gift you ever gave? What made it appropriate for the recipient? _____

_____

_____

A Proper Presentation

Make sure that you wrap the gift with appropriate paper—tasteful all-occasion paper, plain paper, or paper with a suitable sentiment, such as congratulations. Write a short note and sign the card, which should be enclosed in an envelope. Present the gift in person, if possible.

Refusing a Gift

Sometimes you must refuse a gift because it exceeds the monetary limit set by company policy or because the gift itself is inappropriate. In this situation, take the motives of the sender into consideration.

You don't want to embarrass a well-intentioned sender. Be gracious while indicating the problem with the gift. You can say, "What a nice thought! However, since company policy prohibits my acceptance of this gift, I need to return it to you."

If someone has deliberately sent an inappropriate gift—one with sexual overtones or one that comes with an implied business obligation—you want your refusal to tactfully communicate your displeasure at the situation. You can say, "I don't consider this gift appropriate. I am returning it to you," or "This gift is really not appropriate. Please don't send me any more presents."

Accepting a Gift

When you accept a gift, remember to say thank you! Handle the gift with respect. Unwrap it carefully. Admire the gift, if possible. Appear genuinely pleased. Find something positive—or at least pleasantly noncommittal—to say about the gift, such as "How nice of you to think of me!" Write a thank-you note (see Chapter 9).

MIXING BUSINESS WITH LEISURE

The boundaries of acceptable business conduct extend well beyond the walls of your office building. Your co-workers can and will carry judgments about your off-duty behavior into the office arena. When clients are part of the equation, your behavior at social functions reflects on both you and your organization.

■ It's Still Business

The list below includes mistakes commonly made during business social situations. Mark the list with *(P)* for mistakes you may have *personally* made and *(W)* for those you have *witnessed* others committing.

_____ Suddenly began calling the manager or client by his or her first name.

_____ Used inappropriate language.

_____ Failed to attend a mandatory event.

_____ Failed to RSVP.

_____ Didn't include spouses in conversation.

_____ Gossiped or brought up controversial topics.

_____ Didn't assist family members in knowing who staff members were or how to behave.

_____ Didn't send a thank-you note.

_____ Made negative comments about someone's work on a project.

_____ Got drunk.

_____ Consistently failed to attend any informal after-work social gatherings.

_____ Dressed inappropriately.

_____ During a social event, talked only about work.

_____ Acted unhappy to be there.

_____ Didn't compliment or thank the host or organizers.

While we all inadvertently commit faux pas, we need to minimize our mistakes. Each new situation is a new opportunity to improve our performance. Rate yourself again after your next office social event to measure your progress.

Playing for Pay: Entertaining Clients

Taking a client to a symphony concert or a baseball game is not the same as attending an official business meeting, but there is, nonetheless, a hidden agenda. The purpose of the event is to get to know each other a little better outside the formal office environment, not to discuss business. You want the impression you make to be favorable, so that the next time you sit down to negotiate a contract or to place an order, the positive impact of your social time together may provide business dividends.

The following guidelines for conduct with clients are appropriate for many social situations, although the specific applications vary depending on the occasion—a party, a sporting event, or a cultural event (concert, opera, or play).

1. Dress appropriately for the situation while maintaining a professional appearance.

2. Attempt to ensure that the client has a good time. Make transportation and seating arrangements as required. Provide food and drinks.

3. Be knowledgeable about the event you are attending and competent in performing any special skills it requires. React appropriately to performances by artists or players.

4. Use the time to find out a little more about the client—interests, family, and personality.

THE OFFICE PARTY

The annual office party is a command performance if ever there was one. Everyone is there, and most people notice how others are behaving. This is not the time for someone to stand out for his outlandish attire, her distinctive dancing style, or his record-setting number of trips to the buffet.

7

Party Manners

Match the following appropriate behavior with the reason for it; some reasons apply to more than one behavior.

Behavior	Reason behind It
_____ 1. Attend.	A. While it's still business, it's also a party and supposed to be fun.
_____ 2. Be on time.	
_____ 3. Treat your managers with respectful friendliness.	B. You don't want your behavior to haunt you at work.
_____ 4. Look as if you are having fun.	C. It's simply good manners.
_____ 5. Limit talk about business.	D. It's expected and is also a good opportunity for networking.
_____ 6. Don't flirt.	
_____ 7. Don't get drunk.	E. Bringing work into the social setting can make you appear limited in your interests.
_____ 8. Don't gossip or tell off-color jokes or stories.	
_____ 9. Send a thank-you.	

THE THOUGHT THAT COUNTS

A gift, a party, or a night on the town together are all acknowledgments that our co-workers and clients have personal relationships with us extending beyond purely professional connections. These bonds help to keep our work interesting and our psyches stroked. What we are saying by these actions is "I care about you as an individual. I am willing to search for a gift or spend some of my leisure time with you because I want to please you." That's a compliment that goes beyond basic courtesy.

7

Chapter Checkpoints

✓ Carefully consider the appropriateness of a business gift before giving it, paying particular attention to your relationship with the recipient and to the nature of the gift itself.

✓ Remember that a combined business-social event is still business. Your conduct counts.

✓ When entertaining clients, work to ensure an enjoyable experience that reflects well on you and your company.

8 | Managing Dining Dilemmas

This chapter will help you to:

- Effectively plan, schedule, and order a business lunch.
- Understand place settings.
- Provide appropriate tips to waiters, waitresses, and wine stewards.

To get hired at one prestigious law firm we know, it's not enough to have impressive credentials, fine recommendations, and a strong performance in the initial interview. The partner in charge of hiring always makes it a point to take each leading applicant to a fine restaurant for lunch.

From the arrival of the appetizer to the closing cup of coffee, the partner appraises the behavior of the candidate. Woe to those applicants who relax and act inappropriately under the mistaken assumption that the lunch is a mere formality! The partner knows that the way applicants conduct themselves at this lunch shows how they will act in similar situations with the firm's important clients. Those who flunk the "lunch test" do not receive job offers.

Describe the purposes that business lunches serve in your work environment: _____
_____
_____
_____

The business lunch is much more than a meal; it's a test of manners. Careers have been made—and lost—because of lunch manners. However, because so many routine meals are consumed on the run today and because eating out frequently takes place in casual environments, many people lack practice in handling more formal lunch situations. They may not know which bread plate is theirs or which spoon to use.

While business breakfasts are increasingly popular and business dinners also take place, lunch is the meal at which business is most likely to be transacted. Although the same general guidelines apply to both other meals, you may encounter a slightly more formal setting at a business dinner.

APPROPRIATE ARRANGEMENTS

A good business lunch takes planning. If you are the host, you need to do much more than just show up and eat.

The following list can help you prepare for a business lunch. You need to answer *yes* to all of the questions to be properly prepared.

Getting Ready for Lunch

Y   N   **The restaurant is an appropriate setting for a business lunch.**
I have been there recently to check out the food and the service. The atmosphere/ambiance is suitable and professional. We will not be rushed through the meal. We will have time to discuss business.

Y   N   **The situation is appropriate for a business lunch.**
The occasion for the lunch fits within my company's guidelines about the purpose and frequency of business lunches.

Y   N   **The guest has been invited.**
I called the guest a week or two in advance, offering a choice of possible locations, dates, and times.

Y   N   **Reservations have been made.**
        The restaurant knows the number in my party and the time
        of our expected arrival.

Y   N   **The guest knows where we should meet.**
        I have provided clear directions to the restaurant, and I have
        explained where we should wait for each other.

■ Avoiding Awkwardness

You can avoid many of the awkward initial moments in a business lunch
by using suitable business manners. Test your knowledge of appropriate lunch etiquette with the following true-false quiz. The answers are on
pages 101–2.

T   F   **1.** The host—the one who does the inviting—pays for the
            lunch.

T   F   **2.** It's rude to provide a reason for the lunch when inviting
            the guest.

T   F   **3.** A guest should call to confirm the lunch on the morning
            of the luncheon.

T   F   **4.** It's OK to bring someone else along to a business lunch.

T   F   **5.** The host should plan to arrive at the restaurant at the
            same time as the guest.

T   F   **6.** If the guest is more than 10 minutes late, you should call
            her office.

T   F   **7.** Whoever gets to the restaurant first should check his or
            her coat.

T   F   **8.** The maître d' or hostess leads the way to the table, fol-
            lowed by the guest and then the host.

T   F   **9.** The best seat goes to the guest, and the host sits to the left
            of that seat.

T   F   **10.** The host should be prepared to pay for the most expen-
             sive items on the menu.

8

ORDERING COURTEOUSLY

Gracious manners start with the way you order drinks and your meal. Pay attention to the do's and don'ts of restaurant behavior.

Treating Waiters and Waitresses with Respect

Do

- Pay attention to what your waiter or waitress looks like so you can recognize him or her later.
- Catch his or her eye or use a discreet wave of the fingers to request service.
- Address the person by name if asked to do so, otherwise, use *waiter, waitress,* or *server.*

Don't

- Call someone *Sweetie, Garçon, Boy, Dear,* or *Honey.*

- Snap your fingers to get his or her attention.

Ordering Drinks

Do

- As the host, defer to the guest. If the guest orders a drink, order one, too. If he or she doesn't, you should decline. If your guest orders alcohol and you don't want it, order a non-alcoholic drink.
- As a guest, you are advised not to drink alcohol.

Don't

- Push a drink on your guest.

- Have more than one alcoholic drink.

- Pretend to know more than you actually do about wine.

Ordering Food

Do

- As the host, suggest the restaurant's specialties and discuss what you might order to give your guest an idea of the price range of what you're eating. As a host, go to the higher side. As a guest, order in the middle range.

- Let the guest order first, and follow his or her lead. If the guest orders soup or salad, the host should do the same. The same is true for dessert.

Don't

- Badger the waitress or waiter about ingredients and cooking techniques.

- Order foods that are too messy—items like lobster tail, French onion soup, or most forms of pasta.

- Share food.

- Be a picky eater.

DEMYSTIFYING UTENSILS, DISHES, AND GLASSES

8

Place settings can be perplexing! When faced with multiple spoons, forks, and beverage glasses, you may be confused about what's what and what's yours. Once those questions have been answered, you need to know when and how to use each item. In general, the more courses, the more utensils. The most correct, but not the most commonly used, place setting in the United States is based on the idea that you work your way through the utensils, from the outermost one to the innermost one on both sides. When you pause for bites or conversation breaks, put the utensils back on the entrée plate. Never rest the utensils half-on, half-off the plate.

Left-to-Right: The most conventional setting is the one that we learned as children—forks on the left and knife and spoon on the right. The number of utensils can vary. On the left, from the outside in, may be a salad fork and then the entrée fork. On the right, from the outside in, are the dessert spoon and the knife.

Everything in Its Place

Your food dishes, including your bread and butter plate, are to your left. You can recall this by remembering that *food* and *left* both have four letters.

Your drink containers, including your coffee cup, are to the right. Both *drink* and *right* have five letters.

For your utensils, look to the left (four letters) for your fork (four letters) and to the right (five letters) for your knife and spoon (five letters).

MINDING YOUR MANNERS

Basic courtesy is required when eating. Describe a behavior that you consider inappropriate during a meal: _____
_____
_____

Any behavior that is unappetizing is automatically discourteous. Mom was right. Wait for everyone to be served before eating. Don't chew with your mouth open. Chew and swallow before speaking. Take small bites. Don't play with your food or wave it on your utensils. Keep your elbows off the table. Don't comb your hair (or do other grooming chores, including applying lipstick) at the table. Don't talk about gross things at the table. Don't criticize the food. Say please and thank you when passing food.

Some other tips:

- Don't break crackers into your soup or hold a cracker in one hand and the soup spoon in the other.
- Use the flat surface on the edge of your plate to twirl pasta, not the spoon, to avoid messy hanging strands.
- Don't blow on your coffee or soup. Just give hot food or beverages time to cool.
- Don't eat with your fingers. Use a fork to cut French fries into bite-sized pieces as well as to eat bacon and chicken.
- Don't chew ice cubes.
- Cup a lemon wedge in your hand before squeezing it to avoid squirting anyone.
- As a guest, ask permission to smoke. The host should not smoke—or even ask to—unless the guest does. Don't light up until everyone has finished or almost finished dessert and coffee has been served. Cigars and pipes are unacceptable in restaurants.
- Discuss business after ordering. Keep papers off the table until after the entrée plates have been cleared.

8

- Don't push your plate away from you or stack dishes when you've completed your meal.

Handling the Hardware

When confronted with a place setting that confuses you, take your cue from the layout. (See page 98 for an example.) By examining the utensils, you may be able to figure out which is which and thus the order in which you should use them.

If you are still in doubt as to how to proceed, observe others. If you eat just slightly more slowly than they do, you might be able to follow their lead.

If you happen to use the wrong utensil, don't panic or draw attention to your mistake. You can often substitute with the utensil you should have used, or you can quietly ask for a replacement.

8

TIPS ON TIPPING

When the time comes to pay the bill, we suggest you use a credit card. A credit card makes paying quick, easy, and discreet. Then, you also have a receipt for business purposes.

A guest should not argue about who pays the bill. If a man is uncomfortable when the woman is the host, she can say, "Amalgamated Consolidated would really like you to be our guest." The guest should remember to say thank-you! (Within two days, the guest should also send a handwritten note.)

Examine the bill to make sure the tip isn't already included, since this is the practice at some restaurants. For good service, a tip of 15 to 20 percent is appropriate. In formal settings, 5 percent of the total bill goes to the captain (the one who took the order) if there is one. The wine steward gets $3 to $5 per bottle of wine or 15 percent of the cost of the wine. You can leave the money for the tip on the table or include it in the credit card total. Pay the coatroom attendant 50 cents to $1 per coat and the garage attendant $1 to $2.

ENJOYING YOUR MEAL

We take our business lunches seriously—and so should you. When you know and use appropriate table manners, you can better focus on any business that may be discussed. However, it's equally important that you not take lunch manners too seriously. If you accidentally use the wrong fork or drop your napkin, relax! Don't become flustered or overwhelmed and ruin the meal by losing your perspective. With time and practice, your business luncheon manners can become as automatic as any other aspect of your professional behavior.

Answers to true-false quiz from page 95:

1-True. The host—the one who does the inviting—pays for the lunch. It's a good idea to make this clear from the outset. When you issue the invitation, you can say, "Strauss and Thompson would like to take you out to lunch to celebrate the signing of the contract. Would Thursday, the 10th, be convenient?"

2-False. It's polite, not rude, to provide a reason for the lunch when inviting the guest. This helps the guest prepare for any significant discussion. It's also a good idea to let the guest know if anyone else is invited or if there are any materials you'd like her to bring along.

3-False. The host, not the guest, should call the day before or the morning of the luncheon to confirm the lunch with the guest or the guest's secretary.

4-False. A guest should never assume it's appropriate to bring someone else along to a business lunch, because of the added expense for the host. Depending on the purpose of the meeting, you can check with the host ahead of time.

5-False. The host should plan to arrive at the restaurant before the guest rather than at the same time. This allows the host to make sure the reservations are in order and also ensures that he can greet the guest upon arrival.

6-False. You should call the guest's office if she is more than 15 minutes late, but 10 minutes is too soon.

7-False. The host should arrive at the restaurant first and should wait to check her coat until the guest arrives.

8-True. The maître d' or hostess leads the way to the table, followed by the guest and then the host. When there is no hostess or maître d', the host leads the way for the guest.

9-True. The best seat goes to the guest, and the host sits to the left of that seat. In other words, the seat of honor is to the right of the host.

10-True. When you take a guest out to eat, you don't want to worry about money.

8

Chapter Checkpoints

✓ Proper planning can help to ensure a successful business lunch.

✓ Let the place setting be your guide for using utensils. When in doubt, observe others.

✓ Any behavior that is unappetizing is automatically discourteous table manners.

✓ Tip 15 to 20 percent of the total bill.

9 | Expressing and Accepting Appreciation

This chapter will help you to:

- Become more comfortable giving and receiving compliments.
- Know when and how to write a thank-you note.

Jacob Wright, an engineer, was reviewing the plans for construction of the new offices for Kiley Industries with his client, Amanda Kiley, CEO. As they discussed issues ranging from traffic flow to the construction timetable, Jacob took extensive notes on a legal pad, sometimes tearing off a sheet of paper to sketch how an alteration might be arranged.

When the session ended, Amanda Kiley thanked him for his time and input. "By the way," she added, glancing at the notes he had taken, "you have very nice handwriting." Embarrassed, Jacob answered, "Oh, no, I don't. Really, it's just my pen." Amused, Amanda responded, "Well, I have the same kind of pen, and it never made my writing look like that!" ■

Perhaps because of America's Puritan past, many of us have been taught from an early age not only to avoid showing pride in our accomplishments but also to tune out anything that comes close to a compliment. When someone praises a suit or outfit, we may modestly say, "Oh, this old thing!" even if it is a brand new purchase. We know that jealousy and resentment may result from extra attention, so we downplay our contribution to an important project. This deprives us of enjoying the praise we have earned. It also can make people reluctant to give thanks or compliments, since the likelihood that the favorable remarks will be dismissed is very high.

However, it is possible to accept thanks and appreciation without preening or boasting. When you do so graciously, you show respect for the person giving the praise because you are not taking issue with the content of the remark. What's more, there are times when thank-yous and compliments are required, and you should be prepared to give as well as receive them.

Describe the last time you *received* a compliment or thank-you at work:

_____

_____

Describe the last time you *gave* a compliment or thank-you at work:

_____

_____

GIVING AND RECEIVING COMPLIMENTS

In many companies, it's taken for granted that you will do a good job. That expectation doesn't mean that a good job is easy to do. Every day, employees overcome obstacles ranging from working with difficult personalities to solving technological hassles, from enduring constant distractions to making up for insufficient staff, and they still manage to do quality work. For this, they receive a paycheck.

Along with receiving a paycheck, employees need appreciation for jobs that are well done. How frequently this recognition is paid varies within industries as well as with the individuals involved, but some praise should be part of every work environment. When in doubt, people should err slightly on the side of excess.

■ K e e p   U p   t h e   G o o d   W o r k

The number of compliments you give to co-workers reflects your personality as well as your philosophy or management style. On the lines following, match the variations in the way compliments are issued with the likely outcomes. Some outcomes apply to more than one situation.

_____ **1.** Praise comes too late after the event.

_____ **2.** Person doesn't receive expected praise.

_____ **3.** Person who is lavish with praise gives a compliment.

_____ **4.** Person is praised in front of others.

_____ **5.** Person is complimented in front of the manager.

A. The compliment loses some of its impact.

B. The compliment has added impact.

C. The person is insulted.

Perfecting Your Ability to Praise

You don't want a compliment to backfire and make someone feel worse than if you had never issued it. To ensure that your praise has the intended positive effect, take the following steps.

1. *Be consistent.* Compliment everyone who deserves it. If you leave out one individual or one group, even inadvertently, those who are left out are insulted. Also be nonsexist in your reasons for compliments—make sure that you don't compliment women only on how they look and men only on what they do.

2. *Be specific.* It's nice if you say, "That report really seemed like a lot of work." However, it will mean even more if you say, "Breaking out the sales figures by category helped me to see your point about market trends." Being specific can be particularly helpful for those who are

9

reluctant to praise people for fear the recipient may get a big head or for those who want to improve the performance of a problem employee. By praising a specific action, you are making clear exactly what you approve of, rather than issuing a blanket endorsement.

3. *Be direct and eliminate qualifiers.* Go ahead and say you liked something, assuming that you did. Qualifying a compliment, however detracts from it, as in "Pretty good work on the McKenzie presentation."

4. *Don't confuse praise with feedback.* You generally don't want to give a compliment with one hand and take it away with the other. If you say, "You did a fine job on the briefing for the managers. It would have been even better if you had incorporated graphics," your praise loses some of its punch. Allow the person to enjoy your praise and then, the next time he's preparing a report, suggest in advance that he add graphics. Similarly, don't attribute motives to the person you are complimenting. It's insulting to say, "Nice suit. Do you have a funeral or a job interview after work?"

5. *When appropriate, give praise in public or in writing.* The impact of a compliment increases dramatically when it is heard by others or when it is made enduring in writing. Putting praise in writing provides a permanent record and also is good manners.

6. *Be timely.* There's generally no real reason to delay praise. If you delay, you might forget to compliment someone. In addition, it's a basic principle of behavior modification that immediate praise helps someone understand the connection between two events and encourages a repeat performance.

Accepting Acclaim

Many people are so embarrassed or surprised when they receive a compliment that they become flustered in their response. If accepting compliments were an easy thing to do, Hollywood actors and actresses wouldn't need to read those little note cards when accepting their Oscars! Here are some steps to help you with your acceptance speech.

1. *Acknowledge the compliment.* This confirms that you heard what the person said. It should be the first step you take after receiving praise. If you say nothing other than "Thank you," you will have accomplished this goal.

2. *Don't argue with or attempt to qualify the compliment.* If someone says you did a good job on a report, don't say, "Oh, it was nothing," or "Well, it wasn't as good as I had hoped to make it." You're not only putting yourself down but also insulting the person giving the compliment by implying that he doesn't have sufficiently high standards. Instead, you can say, "Thanks, I worked hard on it."

3. *Even when you genuinely disagree with the reason for the compliment, don't insult the speaker.* If you sincerely believe you did a lousy job on the report and are astonished to hear it praised, for heaven's sake, don't say so. Instead, you can say, "I really appreciate your words," or "Your words mean a lot to me."

4. *When possible, anticipate praise and prepare your response.* If you are in a situation in which you can anticipate that you might be praised, take a cue from Oscar winners and think about what you might say in advance. Are there others whose contributions you wish to acknowledge? Lessons you learned from the experience that you wish to share? Try out your response by tape-recording it. How does it sound?

▌Your Turn

Write down the compliments that you would give for the following situations:

1. Martin Wysocki worked many extra hours to fill in for an ill staff member. Without his extra help, you never would have made that deadline last week.

9

_____

_____

_____

2. Susan Bramberg consistently does good work without calling attention to herself. Recently, her job included overseeing installation of a new computer system.

_____

_____

_____

3. Charles Marshall recently agreed to take on the Dunn account, which involves dealing with one of your most important—and finicky—clients. You know that this will be a challenge for him.

_____

_____

_____

Now, write down your response to the following compliments:

4. "You did excellent work analyzing the square footage data in your report on the plant expansion."

_____

_____

_____

5. "I appreciate the delicate way you handled that thorny situation with Morgan. It could have turned into a real problem for us."

_____

_____

_____

6. "Your instructions to the summer interns were right on target. What you said will help all of them to understand their roles and responsibilities."

_____

_____

_____

THE THANK-YOU NOTE

Putting praise or a thank-you in writing makes it into a tangible, enduring expression of appreciation. While many people think of the ability to write thank-you notes as a social rather than a business skill, thank-you notes are both practical and polite in business settings. Even though putting praise or gratitude into writing takes a little effort, usually that effort is greatly appreciated by the recipient.

The Payback Power of Gratitude

Writing a thank-you note is not only a nice expression of appreciation, it is also a smart move from a business perspective. Thank-you notes can benefit your business in several ways.

- *Thank-yous can help to personalize the business relationship.* Sending a thank-you note can make you stand out from the crowd. Your written appreciation casts you in the role of a gracious and thoughtful individual.

- *Thank-yous can help to demonstrate your attention to detail.* When you take the time to write a thank-you note, it shows that you did not overlook the little things. You expressed appreciation for a contribution that otherwise might have gone unsung.

- *Thank-yous can help further good public relations.* You can use a thank-you note as a follow-up to establishing a business contact. A note of appreciation reflects well both on you and on your organization.

    List any other way you can think of that a thank-you note may help you in your business: _____

_____

_____

9

When to Send Thank-You Notes

Timing is crucial with thank-you notes, because they lose their effectiveness rapidly. Ideally, you should send the note within 24 hours of the event that prompted it. The closer to the event the thank-you is sent, the more impact it has.

Several common situations that require thank-you notes follow. Check each category to indicate when you have sent thank-you notes, and then list any additional situations that apply to your business setting.

Y   N   When you receive a gift—from Christmas gifts to wedding gifts to condolence flowers.

Y   N   When you go to lunch with someone such as a new supplier or when you go to dinner at someone's home.

Y   N   When you want to praise an employee or a vendor. The recipients may be your own employees or others who have done work for you. You can also send a thank-you to someone's supervisor.

Y   N   After a job interview or sales call.

Other situations: _____
_____
_____
_____

How to Write a Gracious Thank-You

Many people have trouble thinking beyond the "Dear Aunt Carol" thank-yous of their childhood—those notes your mother may have made you send for birthday or holiday presents. This list of guidelines should help you through most thank-you situations.

1. *If you have legible handwriting, a thank-you note should be hand-written.* Why? The thank-you becomes more personal. However, if no one can decipher your scrawl, type the note so you can get your message across.

2. *Use good-quality note paper.* The paper might have your name and/or company on it, but it should not look too official. Neither should it be cutesy—save those cards for relatives or friends.

3. *Use the recipient's correct name and title.* Make sure you spell names correctly. People are offended if you don't. If you are unsure of a woman's marital status, use her first and last name without a title, as in "Dear Sarah Parker."

4. *Keep your note short.* Many people drag out a thank-you by giving a blow-by-blow account of the event. A thank-you note should be concise. Three to five sentences should do it.

So what do you say, beyond thank you?

- After a sales presentation, you could say, "Thank you for the opportunity to speak with you about our company. I know that we could provide the kind of service you're looking for, and we would enjoy working with you."

- After being rejected for a job or contract, you might say, "Thank you for letting me know of your decision. I hope you will keep my business card (résumé) and consider me for future bids (openings)."

- After a presentation, you can say that it was enjoyable or high-energy and fast-moving, or that it directly addressed the needs of audience.

- After a lunch or dinner, you can comment favorably on the food, the setting, the conversation—or all of them.

- After receiving a gift, you can say; "What a wonderful thing to do. The (item) is beautiful. We love it and will use it often."

5. *Thank everyone who deserves it.* Since word about the receipt of thank-you notes has a way of leaking out, be democratic in your distribution. Leaving someone out of the loop can cause more harm than not thanking anyone. If more than one person needs to be thanked, you can ask the recipient to convey your thanks to others, such as "Please tell your secretary that I appreciate her hard work." If everyone has equal status, send separate notes and make sure they all arrive on the same day. For a dinner thank-you, also thank the spouse.

6. *Use an appropriate closing.* Your closing may be "Sincerely" or "Many thanks again" or "Best regards," but it should convey an appropriately friendly, rather than formal, tone.

7. *Read over the note to check for misspellings, grammatical errors, and omitted words.*

8. *Sign your note, and send it promptly.*

You do not have to send a thank-you for a thank-you. If you choose to do so, you can verbally thank the sender.

Thank-You Tip ─────────────────────────

Establish a file in which you save all the thank-you notes that you receive. Not only is this file a great morale booster, but it can help you when you are "stuck" while trying to write a thank-you of your own. Examine each letter for what made it valuable to you. Was it the way the person was specific? How she commented on multiple aspects of the situation? Expressed the feelings of a group? Acknowledged the time and effort you invested? Apply those aspects to your own notes, and they may write themselves.

 Your Turn

Write a thank-you note for each of the following situations. We did the first one for you.

To thank Sarah Gates, who took you to lunch at the Four Seasons restaurant to celebrate the end of the tax season.

February 5, 1998

Dear Ms. Gates,

Our lunch at the Four Seasons was outstanding. I especially enjoyed the food and your entertaining conversation.

Thank you for a productive meeting. I look forward to doing business with you.

Sincerely,
Marilyn Wise

To Mr. Owens, who sent you and your spouse a crystal bowl as a wedding present.

To Geoffrey Dubois, who allowed you to make a sales presentation to him.

9

To Mrs. Spering, who gave a well-received presentation on leadership to your research and development staff.

WHAT A NICE THING TO SAY

Compliments and thank-you notes have a positive impact on the business environment, inspiring individuals to keep up the good work. Praise provides a good return on a minimal investment. When thank-yous and compliments are well phrased, their effectiveness increases.

9

Chapter Checkpoints

✓ Praise increases in effectiveness when it is consistent, specific, direct, timely, and issued in front of others or in writing. Confusing it with feedback dilutes its impact.

✓ When accepting a compliment, acknowledge that you've heard it. Don't argue with it or attempt to qualify it. Even when you disagree with the reason for the compliment, don't insult the speaker by contradicting him or her. When possible, anticipate praise and prepare your response.

✓ Sending thank-you notes benefits both the sender and the recipient. Send thank-yous within 24 hours of the event that prompted them.

✓ A thank-you should be handwritten on good-quality paper. It should be short and should thank everyone who deserves thanks.

Post-Test

Now that you've worked through *Business Etiquette*, respond to the following statements to assess your current etiquette skills. Congratulations on developing and sharpening these skills!

	Almost Never	Sometimes	Usually	Almost Always
1. I feel confident giving and receiving compliments.	_____	_____	_____	_____
2. I know the proper way to introduce people.	_____	_____	_____	_____
3. I am considered a good listener.	_____	_____	_____	_____
4. I send thank-you notes within 24 hours.	_____	_____	_____	_____
5. I have no difficulty dressing appropriately for business situations.	_____	_____	_____	_____
6. I am not late for appointments.	_____	_____	_____	_____
7. I'm comfortable making small talk with new acquaintances.	_____	_____	_____	_____
8. I use the correct utensils at business lunches.	_____	_____	_____	_____
9. I know how to act at office parties.	_____	_____	_____	_____
10. I sound professional on the telephone.	_____	_____	_____	_____
11. If I'm bringing someone to my office, I know who opens the door and who enters the elevator first.	_____	_____	_____	_____
12. I act graciously when others demonstrate inappropriate manners.	_____	_____	_____	_____
13. My handshake sends a professional message.	_____	_____	_____	_____
14. When someone wants to speak with me, I make sure I don't stand too close or too far away.	_____	_____	_____	_____
15. I regularly evaluate my grooming routine to eliminate gaffes.	_____	_____	_____	_____
16. I feel confident when presenting my business card.	_____	_____	_____	_____
17. I provide appropriate tips to waiters, waitresses, wine stewards, taxicab drivers, and hotel doormen.	_____	_____	_____	_____

	Almost Never	Sometimes	Usually	Almost Always
18. I have a gracious manner when I transfer telephone calls or put people on hold.	_____	_____	_____	_____
19. I refill the paper and reset the copier after I use it.	_____	_____	_____	_____
20. I send faxes only with the recipient's advance approval.	_____	_____	_____	_____
21. When visiting another office, I wait for the host to indicate a chair before I sit down.	_____	_____	_____	_____
22. I give suitable gifts to co-workers on appropriate occasions throughout the year.	_____	_____	_____	_____
23. When entertaining clients, I dress and act appropriately.	_____	_____	_____	_____
24. I respect the privacy of other people's faxes and computer files.	_____	_____	_____	_____
25. I understand why manners matter.	_____	_____	_____	_____
Column totals:	_____	_____	_____	_____
Grand total: _____				

To score: Give yourself one point for each check under *almost never*, two points for *sometimes*, three points for *usually*, and four points for *almost always*. Total each column. Then add the totals of all four columns to get a grand total. How did you do?

100-90   Very good! You are a manners master.

89-75   Good. You are perceived as a polite person.

74-50   Average. You could improve your command of courteous behavior.

49-30   Poor. You need to learn and apply more etiquette skills.

29-0   Very poor. Your behavior offends many people and needs improvement.

Business Skills Express Series

This growing series of books addresses a broad range of key business skills and topics to meet the needs of employees, human resource departments, and training consultants.

To obtain information about these and other Business Skills Express books, please call Irwin Professional Publishing toll free at: 1-800-634-3966.

Effective Performance Management
ISBN   1-55623-867-3

Hiring the Best
ISBN   1-55623-865-7

Writing that Works
ISBN   1-55623-856-8

Customer Service Excellence
ISBN   1-55623-969-6

Writing for Business Results
ISBN   1-55623-854-1

Powerful Presentation Skills
ISBN   1-55623-870-3

Meetings that Work
ISBN   1-55623-866-5

Effective Teamwork
ISBN   1-55623-880-0

Time Management
ISBN   1-55623-888-6

Assertiveness Skills
ISBN   1-55623-857-6

Motivation at Work
ISBN   1-55623-868-1

Overcoming Anxiety at Work
ISBN   1-55623-869-X

Positive Politics at Work
ISBN   1-55623-879-7

Telephone Skills at Work
ISBN   1-55623-858-4

Managing Conflict at Work
ISBN   1-55623-890-8

The New Supervisor: Skills for Success
ISBN   1-55623-762-6

The *Americans with Disabilities Act:* What Supervisors Need to Know
ISBN   1-55623-889-4

Managing the Demands of Work and Home
ISBN   0-7863-0221-6

Effective Listening Skills
ISBN   0-7863-0102-4

Goal Management at Work
ISBN   0-7863-0225-9

Positive Attitudes at Work
ISBN   0-7863-0100-8

Supervising the Difficult Employee
ISBN   0-7863-0219-4

Cultural Diversity in the Workplace
ISBN   0-7863-0125-2

Managing Change in the Workplace
ISBN   0-7863-0162-7

Negotiating for Business Results
ISBN   0-7863-0114-7

Practical Business Communication
ISBN   0-7863-0227-5

High Performance Speaking
ISBN   0-7863-0222-4

Delegation Skills
ISBN   0-7863-0105-9

Coaching Skills: A Guide for Supervisors
ISBN   0-7863-0220-8

Customer Service and the Telephone
ISBN   0-7863-0224-0

Creativity at Work
ISBN   0-7863-0223-2

Effective Interpersonal Relationships
ISBN   0-7863-0255-0

The Participative Leader
ISBN   0-7863-0252-6

Building Customer Loyalty
ISBN   0-7863-0253-4

Getting and Staying Organized
ISBN   0-7863-0254-2

Total Quality Selling
ISBN   0-7863-0324-7

Business Etiquette
ISBN   0-7863-0323-9

Empowering Employees
ISBN   0-7863-0314-X

Training Skills for Supervisors
ISBN   0-7863-0313-1

Moving Meetings
ISBN   0-7863-0333-6

Multicultural Customer Service
ISBN   0-7863-0332-8